On Judging, Conscience and Predestination

Frits Albers, Ph.B.

June 1991

Edited by Frank Calneggia

En Route Books and Media, LLC
Saint Louis, MO

United States of America

ENROUTE
Make the time

En Route Books and Media, LLC
5705 Rhodes Avenue
St. Louis, MO 63109

Contact us at
contactus@enroutebooksandmedia.com

Cover Credit: Dreams of St. John Bosco
by Luigi Morgari (1857-1935)

ISBN-13: 979-8-88870-516-2
Library of Congress Control Number:
Available online at https://catalog.loc.gov

Table of Contents

Table of Contents

Letter from the Author

Now that we Australians are finding ourselves more and more surrounded by evil and hostile forces, we are daily reminded how much in need we are of all the Supernatural protection we can get and how strong the bond is in the 'Communion of Saints' extended to our far-flung shores.

I am happy to have published my latest book which may truly be looked upon as a continuation of its forerunner, the book on "The World Council of Churches". After the publication of that work there appeared in some Australian newspapers – in the aftermath of the diabolical WCC Conference in Canberra in February this year – the revelation of a plot to hijack our beloved Catholic Church in Australia. The plan is to treat it shamefully in isolation from the Universal Church as if it is merely the 'Catholic Church <u>of</u> Australia' (something like 'the Church of England'), the sole property of the local episcopal conference, and then amalgamate it with the local branch of the World Council of Churches in Australia, no doubt as its prize possession, but in reality as its prize captive!

Knowing how intimately the Holy Church is related to Our Blessed Lady as to Her beginning, Mother and Proto-Type, and how far removed from Her the WCC is, I realised with many others that something more must be done to prevent this all-out raid. To show what type of 'catholics' not only envisage, but encourage and support such a deal with Hell, I wrote this little book on Judgement, Conscience and Predestination to further lay bare before my fellow Catholics the inner composition of the Modernists, and why we must never be in awe before them!

Archbishop Cassidy may now be a Cardinal, but his removal from the Papal Secretariate of State must be traced to the same defects which made him take such a large contingent of 'Catholics' to the infamous Canberra WCC conference. We may never be misled by appearances. There is only one moral law for everyone, not one for ordinary Catholics and one for bishops, cardinals or Modernists!

Our Lord did nothing to dispel the utter confusion that reigned in Jerusalem during His trial, when He suffered and died in the execution of the principal task in hand: to wrest control of the world from Satan's grip. The confusion was NOT of His making and would be taken care of when the principal task had been accomplished. Neither is today's confusion the work of the Holy Father, engaged in the same gigantic struggle of Life over Death, to wrest control of the same world from the global forces of Antichrist.

Our Blessed Lady understood, and stayed with Her Son, standing in for each one of us under the Cross as the 'New Eve' of the Redemption. May all Australian Marian Catholics understand the Holy Father and stay with him, fighting with him and under his command the forces of the Underworld in the war zone allocated to their care by Divine Providence, for the good of us all.

Foreword

Starting right back from the earliest teaching days of Her uncompromising Founder and Head, Our Blessed Lord and Saviour Jesus Christ, the Church He founded has always believed and taught that the Redemption won by Christ for the human race was universal, unconditional and absolute. But never, not even 2000 years after this blessed event, has that Church ever taught or believed, that the individual salvation bought by this Redemption extends as far as this Redemption. The Modernist idea that somehow, under God's New Covenant in Christ's Blood, individual salvation must now also be considered as universal, unconditional and absolute, is "the sum-total of all heresies" [Pope st. Pius X]. I have discussed this in greater detail in a previous work entitled "Anatomy of a Modernist".

In vain, as by now they have discovered, did the Modernists appeal for support for their heresy to 'this new church', born from 'the spirit of Vatican II'. In at least four places has this great Council squashed any exhilaration 'that a new catholic church was in the making', by soberly pointing out that the old Catholic Church as we have always known Her is the only One True Church founded by Christ. It is on the basis of their conviction 'that salvation must be believed to be universal', that the Modernists would like to see the Catholic Church stop worrying about 'getting people to heaven', and join the World Council of Churches in the realisation of its 'dream': the founding anew of an earthly paradise of peace and harmony, and freedom from every want, if necessary, by force [Tutu, *et alii*].

But Vatican II has done much more, infinitely more. It has forever ruined the whole monstrous and (needless to say) Modernist idea (the two words mean the same!) that the Catholic Church's claim to uniqueness is an obstacle to ecumenism. Under the direct assistance of the Holy Spirit, this great Council taught the exact opposite! In the two documents in which the Holy Catholic Church reaches out the furthest to embrace the whole world and all its inhabitants in Her crucified love, i.e. in Her "Decree on Ecumenism" and in Her "Declaration on Religious Liberty", the holy Council had no hesitation and no inhibition to show the whole world just

Who it was who was calling all Her separated children to Her UNITY.

The wording of these two Vatican II documents, and even more their impact, is so important that I will not send my readers to go and look them up, just in case they may take my word for it! Here they are. They are just too indispensable for anyone's war against Modernism and against the whole false ecumenism of the World Council of Churches (WCC)! It has every appearance that the Second Vatican Council is saying: "Only Catholics who are anchored to the foundation dogmas of the Church's essential unity, can be safely trusted 'to go out into the whole world and preach the Gospel to every nation'."

> "Nevertheless, our separated brethren are not blessed with that unity which Jesus Christ wished to bestow on all those to whom He has given new birth into one body ... that unity which the Holy Scriptures and the ancient Tradition of the Church proclaim. For it is through Christ's Catholic Church alone, which is the universal help towards salvation,

that the fulness of the means of salvation can be obtained. It was to the Apostolic College alone, of which Peter <u>is</u> the head, that we believe that Our Lord entrusted all the blessings of the New Covenant, in order to establish on earth the one Body of Christ into which all those should be fully incorporated who belong in any way to the People of God."

["Decree on Ecumenism", (3)].

"The sacred Council begins by professing that God Himself has made known to the human race how men by serving Him can be saved and reach happiness in Christ. We believe that this one true religion continues to exist in the Catholic and Apostolic Church, to which the Lord Jesus entrusted the task of spreading it among all men ... All men are bound to seek the truth, especially in what concerns God and <u>His</u> Church, and to embrace it and hold on to it as they come to know it ....

> "The sacred Council likewise proclaims that these obligations bind man's conscience ... So the religious freedom ... leaves intact the traditional Catholic teaching on the moral duty of individuals and societies towards the true religion and One Church of Christ ...
>
> "For the Catholic Church is by the Will of Christ the teacher of truth. It is Her duty ... to declare and confirm by Her Authority the principles of the moral order which spring from human nature itself."
>
> ["Decree on Religious Liberty", (1, 14)].

There is no escape into fairy land: the Catholic Church knows exactly where She stands and what is central to Her universal concern!

In dealing with this whole question of 'the Nature of the One True Church of Christ' in relation to the problem 'to whom belong the elements of truth and holiness found outside Her?', Vatican II has gone much further than the Modernists wish She had, and the sacred Council has settled this matter once and for all.

For 2000 years the Church has taught authoritatively, and Her faithful have always believed, that the Catholic Church is absolutely necessary for salvation, anyone's salvation. So, we could have expected that this Council would have stated 'that the Church founded by Christ EXISTS in the Catholic Church'. However, the Council, in dealing with this very question, used the word "SUBSISTS":

> "This is the sole Church of Christ which in the Creed we profess to be One, Holy, Catholic and Apostolic; which after His resurrection Our Saviour entrusted to Peter's pastoral care, commissioning him and the other Apostles to extend and rule it, and which He raised up for all ages 'as the pillar and mainstay of Truth'. This Church, constituted and organised as a society in the present world, subsists in the Catholic Church, which is governed by the successor of Peter and by the bishops in communion with him. Nevertheless many elements of sanctification and of truth are

> found outside its visible confines. Since these are gifts 'belonging to the Church of Christ', they are forces impelling to Catholic unity."
> ["Lumen Gentium", (8)]

In earlier works, I have argued that this is a fortuitous choice of words. If the Council had chosen the word 'exists', it would then be natural to assume that the Council was teaching that the Catholic Church 'extends as far as She exists': in the visible society of Catholics here on earth. And once again the burning question "to whom belong the elements of holiness and truth found outside Her?" would still not have been resolved. But 'subsists' means more than just 'exists'. It conveys the idea of 'an essential foundation'. And so by using the word 'subsists', the Council can now continue to declare what in fact She did declare: 'that the various elements of holiness and truth found outside the visible confines of the Catholic Church are gifts properly belonging to the Church founded by Christ, and that therefore they possess an inner dynamism to Catholic unity'. This is profound. The Council abstains from telling us what every Modernist has been at pains to tell us, that the bearers of these elements of holiness and truth are MEMBERS of the Catholic Church. But the Council did tell us, that the possessors of these gifts can thank the Catholic Church for their existence. The Catholic Church, while visibly subsisting in the identifiable body of Catholics here on earth, extends invisibly further to give to non-Catholics the elements of truth and holiness they may possess; without making these possessors members of the Catholic Church. Thus, it is that the Catholic Church is essential for non-Catholics, so they can possess the graces necessary for salvation. It is obvious to anyone that the Council has taught us with much greater clarity: where the Catholic Church can be seen to exist, and how far She invisibly extends.

In my previous book *The World Council of Churches*, in the chapter dealing with good priests who, out of fear for their Modernist bishops and fellow-priests, have become soft and silent on uncompromising Catholic Teaching, I charge that their very timidity shows that they are no longer openly and unashamedly in love with the Catholic Church. I did point out that such an attitude plays directly into the hands of those guiding the destiny of The World Council of Churches. The leaders of this body detest nothing more than a Church, which claims for itself to be uniquely founded by Christ, and so regards itself as having been appointed by Christ as the sole possessor and guardian of both the Deposit and the Unity of Faith. It is surely bad enough when Modernists, in their relentless drive for the promotion of the false ecumenism, suppress the above-mentioned clear teaching of the Catholic Church, without good priests adding to the suppression and confusion. Vatican II taught all of us two things very clearly according to even the few quotes used above:

1. Upholding uncompromising Truths in now way harms true ecumenism, Christian unity and religious liberty, and
2. Suppressing uncompromising Truths in now way promotes true ecumenism, true Christian unity and true religious liberty.

The leaders of the WCC reject this out of hand. They are firmly convinced that the opposite is true and they won't have any truck with 'claims to uniqueness', or any Church upholding such claims, using the Modernists' excuse that all this harms ecumenism! They will only consider for membership and accept for amalgamation with their worldwide network 'churches' which do not nurture claims to such exclusive uniqueness. Thus, when Catholics are soft and silent, timid and hesitant, and by now downright confused about the duty, the rights, the wisdom and legality of the Catholic Church to lay claim to that exclusive uniqueness discussed above, then they fly in the face of True Catholicism taught by Vatican II. And they have set the stage for unscrupulous Modernists to combine with a pushy Secretariate of the WCC to spring the trap and hurriedly welcome local amalgamations of the World Council of Churches with this soft and silent, timid and hesitant, confused and doubting slice of Catholicism, the Modernist counterfeit of the Catholic Church.

Going by press reports after my book (*The World Council of Churches*) had been published in MARCH 1991 (after the shambles of the WCC Assembly in Canberra) and after the APRIL 1991 Conference of the Australian Bishops in the Catholic Church, a local 'amalgamation' between the Australian Council of Churches and the Catholic Church in Australia is envisaged, and could be a reality in two years time. The condition for membership is clear: "No claims to individual uniqueness! It is left to the new ecumenical 'church' to decide in this matter".

The Catholic Church of Australia does not exist. No bishop therefore can pretend to have effectively amalgamated the Catholic Church in Australia with the WCC, if the living branch of the Universal Church is being treated as a 'thing' (the Catholic Church of Australia) separate from the Universal Catholic Church, which will never surrender Her claim to uniqueness. This prevents Our Mother the Catholic Church being pushed around at the local level in this whole shabby deal by 'branches' which are prepared to forego Her claim in exchange for whatever ecumenical advantage is envisaged. In essence such advantage cannot be anything but false and vitiated if the Catholic claim to uniqueness is not allowed to be upheld!

After repeated reminders by members of the Church Militant, it ought to be universally known by now that Pope St. Pius X condemns Modernists as apostates. Catholics we see now all around us "laying the axe to the very root, that is, to the Faith and its deepest fibres", and who then "proceed to diffuse poison through the whole tree, so that there is no part of Catholic Truth which they leave untouched, none that they do not stive to corrupt" [1907], can't be anything else. And by this self-same Authority, such Catholics must now be considered "to be no more than a miserable affluent feeding the great movement of apostasy, organised in every country for the establishment of a 'One-World Church'". [1910]: THE most appropriate description for the WCC wishing to amalgamate with the counterfeit church of the Modernists' apostasy. Fear and timidity are the very last things we need in this colossal sham!

Nor do vocal apostates get any sympathy in Holy Scripture. On the authority of St. John, they must consider themselves 'bound for the Second Death' [Rev. 21:8], because, as can be quoted with the authority of St. Paul, 'they did not possess LOVE OF

TRUTH which could have saved them' [2 Thess. 2:10].

But there is no solace for those who, out of a most abject fear for the Modernists, have allowed themselves to be bullied into silence regarding the everlasting, uncompromising, unchanging and necessary Truths of the Holy Catholic Church for which Her Head and Founder had given His Life. For in the list of those bound 'for the Second Death' in one of the passages from the Book of Revelation, St. John puts 'cowards' at the head of everyone else: 'But the legacy for cowards, for those who break their word ... or any sort of liars, is the second death in the burning lake of sulphur' [21:8].

With this book I intend to take the matter further. It never was, and still is not, my intention to chase the Modernists all over the place and into every "dark workshop" [Pope St. Pius X, 1910] into which they crawl to plot against the Church. As always, it is my firm intention to uphold age-old Catholic teaching which alone has power to break the stranglehold of Modernism over Catholic minds and hearts. We received no mandate 'to uproot the cockle' but we did receive from the Cross the everlasting legacy 'to identify cockle' lest it be mistaken for wheat! If, notwithstanding a few notable exceptions, this appears to be no longer the universal practise from pulpits in Catholic churches, from the sees of bishops and the conclaves of their conferences, from the seats of learning in Catholic schools, universities and seminaries, and in the seemingly endless stream of 'catholic' books, periodicals, weeklies, and bulletins at least in the so-called 'civilised West', I make no apologies for exerting my right in the only possible way left to me. The teachings of the Catholic Church on 'judging', 'conscience' and 'predestination' are central to the vital task of identifying the cockle amongst the wheat, or separating false claims from true ones, and of restoring true Catholic confidence in a climate overwhelmed by Modernism and the World Council of Churches. It is still better to light a candle, however small, than forever curse the darkness. Especially if the lit candle is lit in honour of the Blessed Virgin Mary, to whose sacred presence amongst us this modest work is, again, humbly dedicated.

On the Feast of Our Lady Help of Christians.

May 24, 1991.

Introduction

On Judging

One of the most successful ploys the Modernists have used to paralyse all opposition against them has been their incessant cry "Do not judge us!" The utter futility of this plea, made on their own behalf only by themselves to bar any successful attempt at dislodging them from the totally illegal position they occupy in the Catholic Church, and to leave them peacefully in their sin, will be forcefully brought home to them, when after death and before the Judgement Seat of God, they will finally come to realise that the true Catholic teaching on 'judging', known to the Church, already condemned them as criminals and liars while still alive here on earth.

So much can be said about this single topic alone that it will take at least three chapters to cover it adequately for those of the household of the Faith, who can no longer remember having seen or heard it treated in even the briefest of outlines.

Beginning with Catholic Philosophy, which according to Pope Pius XII "chimes in, as by a pre-established harmony, with Divine Revelation" [*Humani Generis*, 1950], and which will give to this whole topic its most enduring foundation (Chapter One), and before turning to Divine Revelation itself: Our Lord's clear teaching on judging in the Gospels (Chapter Three), we will acquaint ourselves with some very startling things St. Paul has to say on judging (Chapter Two), which are so utterly explosive for the untenable position taken by the Modernists, that no doubt they now wish St. Paul had never said them or that no one would dare to draw attention to them. But inspired by the Holy Spirit, St. Paul did make these revelations, if only – as St. Jude puts it in his letter – to give Catholics a chance "to pull even a few from the fire", so they may not hear addressed to themselves what Our Saviour had to say to the Modernists of His own generation 'that they had the devil for their father', and 'that they would die in their sin'.

On Conscience

Modernists claim for themselves and for all their followers the possession of a 'freedom of conscience' to such an impossible degree, that it could quite easily astound even hardened sinners. They are so convinced that conscience (a mere natural light) surpasses in importance the infused and divine gift of Catholic Faith (a supernatural light given for the guidance of the natural light) that we may confidently conclude that they have done away with the priceless gift of Faith and have extinguished its supernatural Light. This whole matter of the proper relationship and interplay between these two lights on our road to Eternity is crying out for proper treatment.

On Predestination

Here is yet another confusion the Modernists prey on in their never-ending search for foul play to consolidate their dominance over the umpire so the 'game' will be played according to their rules. It is well known that Catholics have a quiet aversion, and even dislike, for the word 'predestination' because the totally subversive Protestant input into the meaning and the use of the term has forever wrecked – so it seems – any hope of a proper meaning and use for Catholics. Yet Holy Scripture deals with this whole concept long before Protestantism came on the scene with its twisted application. And the fact that in many places the Bible develops this concept in a forthright manner tells us, that the Magisterium of the Holy Catholic Church is bound to have received from divine inspiration the fullest understanding of the meaning and the use of the term.

It may not be immediately clear to some why anyone should feel impelled to hold to the Catholic meaning of 'predestination' against the Modernist onslaught. Our adversaries rarely if ever use the word, and so it seems a bit far-fetched to accuse them of going against Catholic teaching. The underlying reasoning here is that, if a broad movement such as Modernism does not openly advocate a known false use (the Reformed use) of a term or doctrine, then it is valid to assume that it automatically adheres to the true teaching. Nothing could be further from the truth. To make my point and to show up the fallacy in this reasoning, I shall switch to a know instance when this reasoning becomes unstuck.

All true Catholics know that Protestantism has a totally wrong idea of the Papacy. Now it is true to say that Modernists rarely if ever talk about the Papacy. They don't seem to be openly in favour of the Protestant line, except Paul Collins over the ABC. May we now tacitly assume that Modernism as such possesses the true, sound Catholic teaching on the Pope, and that papal teaching is safe within its ranks? Ninety-one years of total warfare between Orthodox and Modernists have given us the only, true, answer to the query! The fact that the Modernists are totally unconcerned about papal teaching, even dogmatic teaching, means they couldn't care less about the true Catholic doctrine on 'predestination' even if they knew it! But it is a safe bet that they are just as ignorant about it as most Catholics are. And because they are ignorant about this whole question of 'predestination' they are unaware that another error of the magnitude of the Reformed teaching on the subject lies at the root of their own system. And that is the reason why the true Catholic teaching on predestination must be held up in order to refute their fundamental claim: that for the 'Covenant people' (meaning themselves), salvation is secured! It is as serious and as simple as that!

On Judging and Judgements

Chapter One

Foundations in Clear Thinking

Imagine yourself behind the wheel of your car somewhere on a country road, taking your spouse for an hour's drive to your married daughter's place. You are approaching a hill, and after having taken all things into consideration, you think it safe to overtake the vehicle in front of you before the incline. Just as you are about to carry out the necessary manoeuvres, your spouse gives a different appreciation of the situation by yelling: "don't go it darling, you won't make it!" So, you obey and remain behind the car in front doing only 98 km/hr until, after the brow of the hill has been cleared, a new appreciation of the traffic conditions provided an opportunity to decide the next course of action.

Now apply in this everyday occurrence the blanket demand of <u>all</u> the Modernists and their fellow travellers: "DON'T JUDGE!", as if repeating with all the 'veracity' they can muster Our Lord's words in Matt. 7:1 "Do not judge ...". As we know from instinct, from reason and from the sum-total of life's experiences: life as we know it on this planet would cease to exist! One would not be allowed to do what you, the driver in the above-mentioned story had to do, and has done so many times as by second nature: judge the traffic conditions, the relative speed of vehicles, distances, safety aspects, risks, chances etc. One may have a very interesting argument with the person on the left which one of you had the 'right judgement' in this particular case: you in deciding to go 'for the kill'? The other in cautioning against it? You in obeying?, which may never be conclusive until the person on the left of you settles the whole thing with the dry remark: 'You see darling, there was a police car right behind you. If he hadn't booked you for dangerous driving, he would have booked you for speeding while overtaking the car in front of you.' And that, as all motorists agree, is the very last thing we want left for settlement to the 'judgement' of a police officer.

When we come to think of it, a human being makes so many judgments a day, maybe millions, that 'judging' must be part of our make-up, which is the same as saying that this is precisely the way we came forth from the loving hands of our Creator.

Human beings, not having the direct intuition that pure spirits like Angels and demons enjoy, go laboriously through life making endless observations, and carrying out decisions not made so much in the light of the observations, as on the strength of judgements made in between the observations and decisions. This warrants going into more fully.

The human soul, being essentially a true spirit, is immortal and enjoys full possession of intuition. But the human soul is also the life-giving principle of the body, and this intimate link between body and soul during life on earth precludes the full and independent use of that intuition by the Will of the Creator. Thus, the soul, for the acquisition of vital information and knowledge, is forced to go 'outside itself' so to speak to gather information through the five senses of the body, 'the windows of the soul', enjoying a material directness as a kind of 'intuition'. This continuous stream of data is classified and stored by the soul in one of its two main faculties, the mind, and 'temporarily' (i.e. for the duration of its earthly life) stored in the corresponding organ in the body, the human brain. This flow of endless data only becomes KNOWLEDGE when it is classified <u>and</u> stored by the human person in only one way: by means of innumerable JUDGEMENTS.

Since, unlike an animal, the human soul is conscious of this process, and is aware that it is conscious of it, and through this outgoing-and-returning-process discovers itself in reflection, the soul is proven to be a true, living spirit as well as the life-giving form (forma) of the body. A 'first approximation' of Truth is made when it is discovered that the human mind is in agreement, (i.e. in conformity) with the object outside the mind. In other words, when through proper sense-perceptions proper mental images of the object have been formed. If according to St. Thomas my knowledge of a thing matches the thing itself, then I can call that relation 'truth', and my first acquaintance of the object 'truthful'.

But to the same St. Thomas, this is not going far enough. It will help as a first approximation, but even primarily, Truth and Falsehood, according to St. Thomas, lie somewhere else. Truth and Falsehood lie primarily in the JUDGEMENTS the human mind makes about the inter-connections between the myriads of mental images in its store. I may have a true perception of 'Peter' and a true perception of 'white'. But truth is primarily found in the JUDGEMENT: 'Peter is white', which comes about through the linking of a subject 'Peter', with a predicate 'white', by means of the copula 'is'. If this totally mental activity, the linking of a Subject with a Predicate by means of the copula, is true, the knowledge I have of Peter is true knowledge. And until we enjoy the full use of intuition in heaven, this is the only way human beings go about the business of acquiring knowledge: by making true judgements.

The word 'judge', 'judgement', has frightened many people off because of Christ's injunction "Judge not ...". This is unfortunate (and the modernists are making millions out of this confusion, or 'double meaning'), because the same Christ is also the Creator of the human mind, and it is by Divine Will that the human mind simply cannot operate and come to the Truth without making judgements - thousands and perhaps even millions of times a day. We are incessantly linking subjects and predicates all day long, even involuntarily. 'This is my car.' 'It is raining.' 'I must go shopping.' 'Turn the key.' 'Turn left.' 'Slow down.' 'I can just pass him.' 'It is old Mrs Gefoops, slow coach!' 'No, sorry, it's not' ... etc.

As will be better understood after the next two chapters, it is by the Will of Christ that these judgements must also extend to cover people: 'See, I am sending you out as lambs amongst wolves'. 'Beware of false prophets.' 'By their fruits you will know them.' And since Christ cannot contradict Himself, these commands by Christ fall outside His command 'Judge not'. We cannot be commanded by Christ 'to judge the fruits of the Modernists' and then in obedience to that command be accused of disobeying His other command 'Judge not'. We must of necessity study people's sayings, teachings, actions, not only because of Christ's command in the Gospel, but by the Will of the Creator who made us the way we are. To confuse 'judging the actions of people' with 'sitting in judgement over them' is manifestly false and produces the type of paralysis and inactivity the Modernists need so badly to consolidate their grip on the sacred, and to extend their bridgehead within the confines of the City of God. The proclamation of Truth, which by divine injunction must be done, carries with it the open condemnation of the falsehoods of others. And in that way, we show great charity towards sinners if we make known in our defense of the Catholic Church and the Catholic Faith the errors of others which necessitate this defense, so sinners are given an opportunity to repent.

True philosophy, the study of the human being in his environment, not only discovers the truth about the way God the Creator knowingly made us, but also defends the truth of the Gospel, by showing in a marvellous way that there is no contradiction between natural truths, that is, truths which can be ascertained by our human faculties, and Revealed Truths, which can only be ascertained in the supernatural Light of Faith, which cannot be produced by mere human means or efforts. The development of Dogma and the understanding of Faith once given proceed in the same way as the ordinary development of human knowledge: by means of Subject, Predicate and Copula. Supernatural insights are the prerogative of the Holy Spirit, but here on earth they will take, to a large extent and in the ordinary way of things, the form of judgements:

"NO ONE IS GOOD BUT GOD ALONE."

"GOD IS LOVE."

"I AM THE TRUTH, THE WAY AND THE LIFE."

"THE FATHER AND I ARE ONE.'

"BEFORE ABRAHAM EVER WAS, I AM ...."

"... AND HOLY IS HIS NAME."

"TRANSUBSTANTIATION IS A DOGMA OF THE CHURCH."

"CONTRACEPTION IS INTRINSICALLY EVIL ..."

Chapter Two

St. Paul on Judging

St. Paul had no hang-ups. He was not 'conditioned', not even by 'the culture of his time'. He had no scores to settle. He was totally genuine, utterly transparent. He carried his heart on his sleeve because he was openly and unashamedly in love. In love with Christ, in love with the Church.

If ever a saint could be expected to rely on intuition, it was this great Apostle of the Gentiles, "My chosen vessel" [Acts 9:15], inspired by the Holy Spirit. Although a mystic, who could claim to be guided by his visions, there was nevertheless not a trace of 'mysticism' about him. In him, down-to-earthness and common sense became by-words, reaching an all-time high amongst those sent by the Lord 'as lambs among wolves'. In other words, St. Paul lived by his natural and supernatural wits. So, what this man has to say about 'human relations' is worth listening to!

Paul had no illusions about 'the danger of so-called brothers' [2 Cor. 11:26] and the almost irresistible force of being influenced by peer-group pressure and human respect, from which he even had to set free the first Pope, Simon Peter: "When Cephas came to Antioch I withstood him to his face, since he was manifestly in the wrong" [Gal. 2:11]. Paul 'judged' the situation thoroughly. He knew intimately [Acts. 10:1-28 and 15:24] that as far as Simon Peter was concerned, it was not his true attitude, but only a 'pretence' [Gal. 2:13]. He knew how other believers would be watching, would 'judge' the behaviour of Cephas, and would draw their own inevitable conclusion that Simon Peter was teaching by example. Thus the great Apostle of the Gentiles had acquired, from the first moment of his own conversion, a healthy respect for the absolute necessity of 'judging aright'. This is reflected throughout his writings.

When serious differences (even threats of schisms) amongst the early Christians in Corinth necessitated the writing of his first letter to the Church in that city, Paul wasted no time but came straight to the point within the first line after his opening remarks: "Now I beseech you brethren ... that you be perfect in the same mind and in the same judgement" [1 Cor. 1:10]. The last word used here by Paul is **γνωμη**, which the dictionary renders as 'a way of knowing'; 'judgement'.

Judging: 'a way of knowing' - the old Greek knew it from age-old human experience. St. Paul knew it too, not only from human experience, but here directly assisted by divine inspiration. Here then we have direct confirmation that, what we discovered in philosophy, is not being destroyed or rendered superfluous, or even negated, in our new status of 'the new creation' after our elevation from Adam's fall through the Redemption by Christ. The supernatural Light of Faith does not hinder our human 'way of knowing' through judging. Paul insists on it as a first step to sanity in the turmoil in Corinth: 'Judge aright, and judge aright collectively'!

It is as if with this letter St. Paul wanted to expand to such an extent on the meaning and importance of 'judging as a way of knowing', that it turned out to become a whole theology on the Catholic understanding of judging and judgement. Since it was his (and the Holy Spirit's) intention to elaborate on the subject in the body of his letter for all future generations, he makes the fundamental distinction between 'judging'; 'a way to get to know' someone, and 'sitting in judgement' on someone. The remarkable fact is that, in this one letter, he selects HIMSELF for that double 'someone'.

First he says: "Not that it makes the slightest difference to me whether you, or any human tribunal, find me worthy or not. I will not even pass judgement on myself" [1 Cor. 4:3].

Here with the word 'worthy', St. Paul completely reveals the judging, which according to the mind of Christ, may not be done. Judging the 'worthiness' of someone is akin to 'sitting in judgement' on him. St. Paul clearly states that, by not judging his own worthiness, he is not sitting in judgement on himself. This ultimate in judgement must be left to God.

So it is not so strange that after that, and in that very same letter, he tells the Corinthians, and all the Churches for that matter, just how far we can go before we sit 'in judgement' on one another. To make that clear he instructs them to do something, which on first sight appears to be the exact opposite: he tells them to judge him: "I say to you as sensible people: judge for yourselves what I am saying" [10:16]. Clearly, he says here: 'Not to judge in that other, that second sense IS NOT SENSIBLE'. You are not being sensible if you refuse to judge carefully people's sayings, teachings, actions, even those of St. Paul! The difference is so fundamental that the Apostle could only drive it home by referring both applications to his own person: the way <u>not</u> to judge Paul, which is futile and sterile, and the necessary and <u>sensible</u> way to judge him: the way that leads to true and desirable knowledge as a guide for action.

The immediate necessity for all this springs to light when in this selfsame letter he uses this teaching for a practical application, when he directs the Church in Corinth 'to throw out a known and unrepentant sinner of the worst kind'. Once that matter had been cleared up, Paul elaborates on the matter of judging. Apparently, the Christians of Corinth 'had not been very sensible' in not judging carefully what he had been telling them to do. So now he was forced to correct erroneous assumptions as the result of this neglect. I hand you over to St. Paul:

> "When I wrote in my letter to you not to associate with people living immoral lives, I was not meaning to include all the people in the

world who are sexually immoral ... What I wrote was that you should not associate with a brother Christian who is leading an immoral life ... you should not even eat a meal with people like that ... OF THOSE WHO ARE INSIDE YOU CAN SURELY BE THE JUDGES" [1 Cor. 5:9-13].

Although Modernists according to Pope St. Pius X are definitely 'on the outside', they nevertheless consider themselves to be wholly 'on the inside', swarming all over the place. And so, according to the Holy Spirit here, it is mandatory that their sayings, teachings and actions must be judged by those on the inside so as to see if they must be avoided 'even to the point of not eating with them'.

Still the Apostle is not satisfied, and thus he takes this whole matter of judging even further. And still in the back of his mind is the great danger of schisms as the sorry aftermath of Christians not being 'sensible': not being critical and alert enough in essentials.

The Apostle now turns his attention to tribunals. At the time of writing, the Corinthians must have been in the grip of the same plague that is sweeping the Western world of our times: the lust for litigation and get-rich-quick the easy way. Back to St. Paul:

> "How dare one of your members take up a complaint against another in the lawcourts of the unjust instead of before the Saints? As you know, it is the Saints who are to judge the world; and if the world is to be judged by you, how can you be unfit to judge trifling cases? Since we are also to judge Angels, it follows that we can judge matters of everyday life. But when you have cases of that kind, the people you appointed to try them were not even respected in the Church."
>
> [1 Cor. 6:1-4].

Once again, the poor Corinthians had it all wrong. Instead of them 'judging the world' they allowed the exact opposite to happen according to St. Paul (and the Holy Spirit): 'they allowed the world to judge them'! Since this quote is bristling with the word 'judge' in all sorts of meanings, it has been made abundantly clear (i) how far from timid was St. Paul in using it; (ii) how positive the effects are the Apostle expects from the acceptance and implementation of his teaching on judging, and (iii) how positively alarming the consequences are if Christians are too frightened to 'judge' this teaching for themselves and put it into practice. How alarming?

Let us turn to Our Lord.

Chapter Three

Our Blessed Lord on Judging

In turning to Our Blessed Lord's teachings on 'judging' and 'judgement' in the Gospels, we not only come before Our Redeemer, but we also find ourselves then in the presence of our Creator. From the teachings of a philosophy, on which the Holy Catholic Church has placed Her stamp of approval by officially declaring 'that it chimes in, by a pre-established harmony, with Divine Revelation', we learn that the human mind progresses in knowledge by the seemingly endless activity of 'judging' as explained in Chapter One. We can now be absolutely certain that our Divine Master did not with one stroke destroy His Father's creation and His own handiwork, when He gave the members of His Church the command "Judge not ...", something the Modernists would love us to believe for their own short-term gain but eventually also for their everlasting downfall.

From the writings of St. Paul, inspired by the Holy Spirit, we know the difference between 'judging other people' and 'sitting in judgement over other people'. St. Paul would not even 'sit in judgement over himself', but he most certainly wanted Christians to judge the behaviour, the works, words, sayings, and actions of other people, including himself, in order to see for themselves how to react to them, even, if necessary, to see if they had to go as far as to dissociate themselves from other Christians. And he most certainly put into practise himself what he required of others. The cohesion of the New Testament demands that this teaching on judging and judgement (including the necessary consequences of dissociation!) is not only in a kind of loose agreement with what Our Lord has said, and may not only be viewed as Paul's personal opinion of what Our Lord may have meant, BUT ACTUALLY AND DIRECTLY COMES FROM HIM! As is to be expected, there will be no trouble in showing the existence of this natural and supernatural bond. St. Paul had read and understood Our Blessed Lord accurately and reflected His teaching faithfully, not only the spirit of it, but to the letter!

We will start a discussion on Our Lord's teaching on judging with what has already been mentioned a few times so far: in what context did Our Lord give the command "Judge not"? St. Matthew tells us in Ch 7. V. 1.

"Do not judge and you will not be judged."

The 'you' here is personal, going directly to the owner of all the outward manifestations: actions, sayings, works and behaviour, by which human beings make known their inner self, and which Our Lord knows will remain the legitimate object of other people's observations. So Our Lord clearly tells us here:

"Do not sit in judgement over the <u>owner</u> of all the outward manifestations, and then 'you' i.e. your personal self, 'your own ownership' will not be in question, and will be respected until judged by Me. Even if My people will have to disapprove of the <u>use</u> you make of that ownership in your outward manifestations to such an extent, that you have become a danger to their eternal salvation, so that on My command they will have to dissociate themselves from you." This ownership, and the unseen <u>value</u> of its personal use, must be left to the judgement of

God. But the way it is being used, and the impact it has on others, is open for scrutiny just as everything else in this life.

Our Lord's use of the word 'hypocrite' in the context of His teaching on 'judging' sheds further abundant light on what He considers definitely legitimate, and so included in the foundations for His future teachings on judging, brotherly correction and segregation: all forms of 'hypocrisy' are proper objects for judgements!

Carefully observing Our Lord's choice of words here we cannot fail to notice the absence of words He did <u>not</u> say. For obvious reasons He did not tell His followers: "Do not judge the words and actions, the works, behaviour and all other outward manifestations of your fellow men, and then yours will not be judged". Not only would it be impossible to exact and expect adherence to such an injunction from creatures He Himself had created as such a strong unity between body and soul: such a demand would also fly in the face of His follow-up teaching on judging as will be seen shortly. Such outward manifestations (i.e. words, teachings, actions, behaviour, works, etc.) are therefore <u>not</u> part of what

He is teaching here on 'sitting in judgement', even if Modernists insist, for the success of their own evil purposes, that we must consider this to be the case.

Leaving to my readers to assess for themselves the amount of ordinary, everyday 'judging' (even agonising 'judging'!) needed to comply with some well-known sayings of Our Lord:

- "Be circumspect like snakes". (Not just once a year!);
- "Beware of the yeast of the Pharisees". (At all times);
- "If your brother sins against you ..." (70 times a day);
- "When you see Jerusalem surrounded by armies ..." (What did the Master say had to be done?);
- "Beware of false prophets who come to you disguised as sheep, but underneath are ravenous wolves" (A life-time's job);
- "Beware of men: they will hand you over ..." (Same again);

- "Do not cast your pearls before pigs." (How does one know who are the pigs except by careful study and sifting?);
- "If your eye causes you to sin, pluck it out.";
- "If anyone comes to Me without hating his father, mother, wife, children, brothers, sisters, yes and even his own life too, he cannot be My disciple." (Imagine the agonising over that one.)

We will go immediately to "the fruits and trees": the heart of Our Lord's teaching on judging.

Our Lord's teaching on 'judging the fruits of the trees' and 'judging the trees themselves by their fruits' is found in the Gospels of St. Matthew [7:15-20] and St. Luke [6:43-45]. First the version of St. Matthew.

> "Beware of false prophets who come to you disguised as sheep but underneath are ravenous wolves. You will be able to tell them by their fruits. Can people pick grapes from thorns, or figs from thistles? In the same

> way, a sound tree produces good fruit but a rotten tree bad fruit. A sound tree cannot bear bad fruit, nor a rotten tree bear good fruit. Any tree that does not produce good fruit is cut down and thrown on the fire. I repeat, you will be able to tell them by their fruits."

On the surface, straightforward teaching, clear thinking. Nothing exceptional or out of the ordinary, except that, when applied (as Our Lord insists here) to living people, most Catholics seem to have at least two insurmountable problems with it, if we may go by the very large number of them who simply and thoughtlessly not only tolerate ravenous Modernists, but follow them! The first problem is that a staggering number of them will not even 'judge the fruit'. Our Lord insists that they do (for obvious reasons); the Modernists insist that they don't (again, for obvious reasons). By disobeying Our Lord for fear of going against His command: "Do not judge ...", they achieve the very things the Modernists want, and for which St. Paul berated the Corinthians under the direct inspiration of the Holy

Spirit: they fall into schisms by allowing Modernists to lead them away from the Faith. 'Fruits': words and sayings, actions, behaviour, life-styles and arguments must be judged, when offered by the peddlers of 'religious wares' as dutifully as when offered by any other flim-flam man, even if the peddler occupies the pulpit. Like any other cheat, Modernists are completely silent on the deficiencies of their wares! RENEW was and remains the classic example of this!

Not satisfied with this, Our Blessed Lord insists that we go further and 'judge the tree by its fruits'. And here He probably lost 95% of all twentieth-century Western Catholics, because, even if some of them dare to judge the 'fruits' of the Modernists, they stop short of 'judging the tree', because they are by now convinced that 'the tree is somehow the man' and they cannot see their way clear of judging the tree without judging the man. Unfortunately, this reasoning, though very profitable for the Modernists, is at the same time very insulting for Our Blessed Lord, as if He doesn't know what He is talking about. Our Lord insists: 'Do not judge ...', and He is equally insistent 'that we judge the tree by its fruits'. So, obeying His command 'to judge the tree by its fruits' cannot possibly impinge on His other command: "Do not judge ..." And to wrong-foot all these soft-hearted Catholics even further, judging, according to Our Lord, is not to stop even here. We still haven't reached 'the man'. There is still more judging to be done after we have identified the 'tree by its fruit'. And even then, in that very advanced next stage, we are still not, according to Our Lord, 'judging the man' if we do exactly as He tells us. And anyone who has pondered over what His great Apostle St. Paul taught us on the subject will know what comes next.

We have already said that St. Paul read Our Lord accurately and dared to take Him at His word! And Modernism never would have made the inroads into Catholicism as it has done in our days, if all Catholics had taken this teaching of Our Blessed Lord to heart! But first let us settle the question of 'judging the tree by its fruit' - a bridge that must be crossed safely if we are to arrive at the so vital understanding, needed to heed Our Lord's further instruction on what we do next after we have identified the 'tree'.

Our dear Lord knew what a difficult thing this whole duty of 'judging' is, which He had been required to impose on His followers 'according to the request of His Father' [Jo. 3:11; 17:8]. Had we only been given this part of St. Matthew's Gospel on this subject of judging, most Catholics would have been able to acquire a satisfactory understanding of 'judging the fruit', enough even for the more adventurous ones to put the command into practice. But the question of the 'tree' would have been beyond most of us. So, we must be grateful that He gave to His Church the conclusion of this teaching in St. Matthew's Gospel in Ch. 12, to which has been added the precision of St. Luke in Ch. 6. Both Gospels hand us the key which opens the door on this whole abstruse question of 'recognising the tree'. First, here is St. Matthew's version:

> "Make a tree sound, and its fruit will be sound; make a tree rotten and its fruit will be rotten. For the tree can be told by its fruit. Brood of vipers, how can your speech be good when you are evil? For a man's words flow out of what fills his heart. A good man draws

good things from his store of goodness; a bad man draws bad things from his store of badness. So I tell you this, that for every unfounded word men utter, they will answer on Judgement day, since it is by your words that you will be acquitted, and by your words condemned." [Mt. 12:33-37].

And here is the precision added by St. Luke: "There is no sound tree that produces rotten fruit, nor again a rotten tree that produces sound fruit. For every tree can be told by its own fruit. People do not pick figs from thorns nor gather grapes from brambles. A good man draws what is good FROM THE STORE OF GOODNESS IN HIS HEART just as a bad man draws what is bad from the store of badness. For a man's words flow out of what fills his heart." [Lk. 6:43-45].

So there we have the simple distinction between 'the man' and 'the tree'. The tree is not the man: the tree is 'the store that is in a man's heart' and that can be judged, and must be judged aright (if we are to fulfil Our Lord' command) from what the man says and does without necessarily sitting in judgement over the owner of the store: the man himself. And we can round off our understanding and complete the picture, by taking into account the realistic observation made by Our Lord in Lk. 12:34 and Mt. 6:21 "For where your treasure is, there will be your heart also".

Now we know what bad trees Teilhardism, Modernism, and RENEW are from the rotten things (fruits) they make our Modernist bishops and priests, teilhardian nuns and teachers, and our RENEWed Catholics say, do and write. And here we are not only taught that these things come 'from their hearts', but now we know also with divine assurance that we may judge that the tree producing these outward manifestations is 'treasured' there in those hearts! The tree then, this 'treasure in the heart', is the accumulation of teachings and learning, opinions and conclusions, desires and life's experiences stored up in a man's heart as a treasure, from which the man, according to the Maker of man's heart, produces his fruits in words and actions.

The way has now been cleared to come to the crux of this whole teaching, and for us to begin to appreciate why Our Blessed Lord calls this treasured store in man's heart a 'tree'. We all know how impossible it is to uproot and transplant an old tree. Here then, Our Lord has brought us face-to-face with all education, and especially with education in the Catholic Faith: the formation of young 'trees' in young children. And not only are we faced here with the overriding importance of Catholic education as such – maybe even more importantly – with the ASSESSMENT of that education: the testing and judging of the 'fruits'; with the necessary demand for an early re-education if the 'fruits' are judged unsatisfactory.

With this Divine assurance of the strong link between the 'tree and its fruits', between education: the planting of the 'tree', and the valuable art of assessment: the necessary testing of its 'fruits', we have come to the root-cause of the evil of Modernism. For it is to the everlasting damnation of Modernism, that the unique Catholic education in schools and seminaries, together with its indispensable assessment, have been destroyed in Australia with the active cooperation of bishops and priests, teachers and parents! To such an extent that the true Catholic Faith can now only be taught surreptitiously in 'catholic' schools by a dedicated few to a lucky selected minority. According to our Divine Master, Modernism must now be judged to be at home as a treasured, fully-grown tree in the hearts of those capable of inflicting such a massive supernatural tragedy.

What next? What is to be done now, after the tree of Modernism has been identified in the hearts of so many RENEWed bishops and priests, nuns and teachers, parents and 'theologians' by the visible fruit of anti-Catholic behaviour displayed by them?

Our Lord has still left us plenty of room to manoeuvre without us breaking His command: 'Do not sit in judgement!'

Modernists still fall under His universal command of Love, but outwardly applied in a somewhat different way than is usually accepted, in order to have the greatest possible impact: effects, that is, of conversion. Our Lord, St. John and St. Paul literally concur in this very serious matter of what is to be done next; especially, but not exclusively, in the case of the worse possible scenario. And the two greatest theologians among the Apostles have taken their cue from the Master, that the worse possible scenario is that 'of leading others astray'. Our Lord himself brought up this subject as a fact of life in chapter 18 of St. Matthew's Gospel, and with the words quoted in the following extract He has indicated how this distasteful matter must be seen through:

> "If your brother sins against you (said in the context of 'leading others astray', but not necessarily restricted to this extreme case) go and have it out with him alone between your two selves. If he listens to you, you have won back your brother. If he does not listen, take one or two others along with you: the evidence of two or three witnesses is required to sustain any charge. But if he refuses to listen to these, 'DIC ECCLESIAE': 'tell the Church'. If he refuses to listen to the Church, treat him then like a pagan or a tax collector." [Mt. 18: 15-17].

To a man, the Modernists have refused to listen to the Church after maybe millions of individual and collective approaches made by Catholics on behalf of themselves and of their children the world over. In how many cases have these Modernists, these false but popular prophets "because they leave 'My people' in their sins", been judged 'to lead others astray', and have they been shunned as pagans and tax collectors on Our Lord's express command? Going by all that spontaneous handclapping, backslapping and excitement in churches during the concelebrated Masses in addition to the expensive presents given to Modernist priests every time they finally condescend to move on, the opposite is true: they are not shunned as counterfeit: they are hailed as the genuine shepherds! Not only are these catholics prepared to eat themselves sick on the poisonous fruits of the trees supplied by the Modernists, they show no love for the Modernists. The shunning was meant by Christ as a last attempt at 'uprooting the tree' and seeing it 'burnt up' in the collective Love of the Catholic Church here on earth before both tree and owner are finally condemned to burn uselessly in the everlasting flames of Hell! "Any tree that does not produce good fruit is cut down and thrown on the fire." It is of the utmost importance WHICH fire: the 'fire of love' here on earth, kept alive by those who genuinely love their enemies, a fire that burns dead wood and leads to salvation. Or the other fire shown by Our Lady of Fatima to three innocent children, capable of setting their little hearts alight with the flames of that first fire, a burning love for poor sinners, strong enough to burn up every rotten tree in men's hearts that does not produce good fruit, before it is too late ....

As already stated, both St. John and St. Paul have shown us in their writings that they concur with the reasons for Our Lord's drastic demand for the isolation and shunning of those brothers who lead others astray. In giving their own version of Our Lord's injunction, they see it not only as a safeguard for others, but also as the final act of Love to very unfortunate Catholics. In order that the local and immediate shunning has the desired effect intended by Divine Love, it must be adhered to in all its strictness. It may not be viewed by anyone for instance, as 'sitting in judgement' over the owner of the infested orchard. It remains the simple execution of a necessary quarantine, the quiet decision of having nothing further to do socially with the owners of the diseased trees. Also, it must not be inconsistent or temperamental, subject to 'the way we feel' from day to day. And finally, it better remain an individual decision, open to review, taken on the authority of Our Lord Himself, and on the insistence of both St. Paul and St. John.

We remind the reader that we gave an abridged form of St. Paul's version in Chapter Two of this book. What St. John has to say on the matter of avoiding those who lead others astray can be found in the Apostle's Second Letter and follows here:

> "If anyone brings you not this Gospel, receive him not in your house. Do not even greet him lest your greeting makes you a partaker in his wicked work." [10-11]

So that is what Our Lord meant when He left us with the command: "Treat him like a pagan and a tax collector", when someone is leading others astray by not bringing them 'this Gospel':

- ‘Receive him not in your house.’
- ‘Refuse to have a meal with him.’
- ‘Do not even greet him ...’

If applause, backslapping, greeting and handshakes, meals, outings, parties and invitations are all indications of encouragement and of social acceptability, then a personal rebuff as the surest short-cut to a necessary soul-searching has a devastating effect which rankles forever. The classic example of this, inspired by the Holy Spirit, can be found in the Book of Esther of which the compelling details will be quoted now. A certain Haman had been plotting with two high officials at the court of the Persian king to assassinate him. The plot was thwarted by Mordecai, a Jew. The implication of the two officials came to light but not yet the involvement of Haman.

The short Prologue of the book acquaints us, by way of Mordecai’s dream, with its central theme: the plan to exterminate all the Jews, and briefly outlines the reason for this revenge: the plot and execution of the high officials. It concludes with the final remark: ‘The king then appointed Mordecai to an office at his court and rewarded him with presents. But Haman, son of Hammedatha, who enjoyed high favour with the king, determined to injure Mordecai in revenge for the king's two enuchs'. Now read on:

> "Shortly afterwards King Ahasuerus singled out Haman for promotion. He raised him in rank, and gave orders that all the officials employed at the Chancellery were to bow down and prostrate themselves before Haman. Mordecai refused either to bow or prostrate himself ... When Haman had seen for himself that Mordecai did not bow or prostrate himself before him, he was seized with fury. Having been told what race Mordecai belonged to, he could not be content with murdering Mordecai, but made up his mind to wipe out all members of Mordecai's race, the Jews, throughout the entire empire of Ahasuerus ...."
>
> "Haman left full of joy and in high spirits that day; but when he saw Mordecai at the Chancellery, neither standing up nor stirring

> at his approach, he felt a gust of anger ... Returning home he sent for his friends and his wife, and held forth to them about his dazzling wealth, his many children, how the king had raised him to a position of honour, and promoted him over the heads of the king's administrators and ministers ... 'But what do I care about all this when all the while I see Mordecai the Jew sitting there at the Chancellery'?"

The rest is history. Instead of Mordecai, it was the plotter Haman who was finally turned down and out, suspended from the gallows he had erected for the man he hated because he dared to ignore him in public ...

When we hear from pulpits (and what follows now has been said in my presence) how incomprehensible it is 'for us, modern Catholics' that in the past the Church could have sunk so low as to haggle about if the Holy Spirit comes forth from the Father or from the Father and the Son, and if Christ is present in the Eucharist by means of Transubstantiation or by whatever means, and that the old ecclesiology is now dead and that instead the deaneries are the highest authority in the 'local churches', then we know for sure from this public profession of unbelief in Catholic Dogmas, that in such priests Catholic Faith has been uprooted, and has been replaced by the deadly tree of Modernism during the disastrous stay at the 'seminary'. And these are now 'leaders' who push for the amalgamation of their 'local churches' with the World Council of Churches, since their local 'church' no longer claims to be part of the unique Catholic Church, but claims to be autonomous from Her, i.e. entitled to make such decisions. Obviously, this is the way any 'deal' will be hailed and interpreted, which any federation of local catholicism will make anywhere with any National Council of Churches: as the successful local achievement of the inexorable drive of the World Council of Churches to finally 'possess' and dominate the Catholic Church!

And on whose 'authority' do these Modernist priests contradict Our Lord, and beg us not to judge their fruits and their trees, their drives and their decisions? On no other authority than that of "the father of lies", who wants them to remain in their sin.

For the devil knows that the Divine recipe for proper judging all the way to the quarantine not only leads to safeguarding the faithful but has the additional purpose of leading the sinner to the beginning of all conversion: a healthy rethink, the way of the prodigal son "come to his senses when no one gave him anything".

If Haman's downfall and the rescue of the Jews were precipitated by the uncompromising stand of two individuals (and by the infallible inspiration of the Holy Spirit we learn that Esther and her custodian Mordecai judged the situation aright) then we know for certain that a similar display of right judgement and public courage will become the same instrument for Divine intervention on behalf of our fellow Catholics. We have the inestimable support of a Divine command, with Apostolic confirmation, to treat people who lead others astray and who will not listen to the Church, as tax collectors and sinners. Such powerful teaching was denied to Mordecai and Esther, but in no way did the absence of it affect their display of a natural as well as a supernatural right judgement and subsequent behaviour. At the same time, we must admit to our sorrow and shame, that the presence of this powerful teaching in our redeemed environment is no guarantee that it will be adhered to! We Catholics in Australia will have barely two years to judge if the 'ecumenism' envisaged by the WCC and their Modernist friends is the same ecumenism envisaged by the Holy Spirit and communicated by His Bride, the Holy Catholic Church. We will not leave you in the dark in this matter of global importance.

On Conscience and Conscience Formation

Chapter Four

Some Necessary Preliminaries

At the end of the previous chapter, I sounded the Catholic Church's warning of the enormous consequences once Catholic Faith has been uprooted and has been supplanted by whatever other 'faith'. When that calamity overtakes a Catholic, the priceless gift has been lost forever. This pearl of great beauty was once given as an absolutely free gift from God as God's greatest gift to finite little man, but once rejected, it will never be restored by the ordinary economy of Grace available to the Church. It can only be revived by a miracle of Grace, and God is not bound to perform a miracle. This stark reality is bedrock in any discussion on 'conscience'. And if, in 1910, Pope St. Pius X had reason to enlighten the Holy Church about the full scale operation in every country of concerted efforts towards the establishment of a great movement of apostasy, that is, an exodus away from the priceless gift of Catholic Faith, then now, 81 years later, we know exactly what he was talking about! For Catholics, an appeal to conscience in disregard, contradiction or even the total loss of Catholic Faith is as useless as an appeal to an idol! The widespread practice by Catholics of holding up their freedom of conscience to use contraceptives ["The Mark of the Beast"] against the infallible teaching of *Humanae Vitae* has proven to be a disaster of the first magnitude, not only for Western Catholicism as such, but in the wrecking of one individual life after another!

For Catholics, no discussion of conscience is helpful without a good understanding of Catholic Faith. Due to the diabolical efforts of the ever-present Modernists and their equally persistent support groups and timid yes-persons, the understanding of vital aspects and content of Catholic Faith has plummeted to an all-time low, in many young Catholics even below the level of consciousness, to become embedded somewhere in the subconscience. The first requirement, therefore, is that Church teaching relating to Catholic Faith must be properly brought out, before a discussion can take place on the inter-relationship between Faith and conscience. That explains the heading of this chapter.

Most of us may know of the harrowing experience of being aboard an aircraft forced to land in thick fog. While some of his passengers' faith in 'guiding Angels' is revived and found to be most comforting in such a moment of anxiety, the pilot's faith – apart from probably sharing that of his passengers in the helping Angels – is nevertheless at this moment of a different orientation and preoccupation. His faith in the safety of his passengers hinges entirely on his faith in the accuracy of his instrument panel and his electronic equipment. If he has no doubt about the latter, then there is no room for doubt about his aircraft's safety. True, he is only safe from a collision if he flies higher than the highest obstacle in his path. The height of the plane is the only reality that counts. He has no direct, intuitive knowledge of the actual height of his aircraft: the reality that matters. But this reality remains hidden from him: he still cannot see the actual height of his plane. It all hinges on the evidence available to him with regard to the reliability of his instruments in recording faithfully for him the true reality of his plane's position, which is a great good for him and his passengers.

Such a common everyday example shows that 'faith' is far more widespread, and a far more 'basic commodity', in human life here on earth – even among scientists! – than people are prepared to give it credit for. Like 'judging', it is an absolute essential in the pursuit of knowledge, which is the same as saying once again that it is yet another fascinating way we come forth from the loving hands of the Creator. We are forced to make as many 'acts of faith' a day as we make judgements: maybe millions of times. And we would not even know it! And all this, because our explicit intuition which our soul possesses as a true spirit, is reduced to an implicit function as long as here on earth our soul is forced to act through matter: through the body and its five senses. But all the necessary ingredients for the basic understanding of an act of supernatural, infused, divine and Catholic Faith are all present in the little example of everyday faith quoted above. Let us begin, then, the interesting analysis of those basic ingredients.

Initially, the three basic ingredients for 'an act of judgement' are essentially the same as for 'an act of faith'. We need a living, enquiring human brain which has some concept called 'a subject', in our earlier example 'a man called Peter'. We need some concept of another reality, called an object, the existence of which we have become aware of independently of this first concept, in our example 'white'. And now we link the subject with the object by means of the copula 'is', to make ONE judgement 'Peter is white'. If this judgement of Peter is in conformity with the reality outside us, we call the judgement true.

Now go back to the pilot with his plane in dense fog, trying to land the passengers in safety. Here is certainly a living, enquiring human brain with all sorts of concepts needed for the job. Outside him is the reality he is fully aware of but cannot see: the height of his plane. And right between him and that outside reality, like a kind of 'copula' or 'link' is an instrument called an altimeter. And from 'faith' in the reliability of his instrument, and not from direct intuition, he now makes the true judgement: 'the plane is on a safe height'. Via the instrument he is in a knowing and confident contact with the unseen reality. The contact is direct, the knowledge is sure, but the 'vision' of the reality still remains indirect.

For sure and confident, even accurate knowledge, the vision is not an immediate requirement. But we must realise that even the acceptance of the truth of the judgement 'the plane is on a safe height' is itself 'an act of faith': we still don't possess direct, intuitive knowledge of truth. But that does not prevent us from <u>knowing</u> with certainty that the judgement <u>is</u> true. This explains the truth of the previous statement: that all our 'acts of faith' extend as far as our 'acts of judgement'. We trust our judgements to be true, even if we are so sure that we are prepared to swear on that!

To broaden the picture without any essential alterations, we will now look at some of the well-known replacements we have for 'the link in the middle': in our example, the instrument. In an act of faith, the common name for 'the link in the middle' is 'symbol' or 'sign'. On the one hand, we always have an enquiring mind. On the other hand we always have myriads of 'unseen realities'. And in between these two, making the desirable link between the mind and the unseen reality, is always a third: a symbol or sign in the form of (a) a teacher; (b) an authority; (c) a spoken word; or else a document, a book or newspaper; or (d) an instrument: TV, radio, altimeter, etc. In <u>all</u> these cases, it is the reliability of 'the symbol in the middle', which induces faith in the symbol itself, stretching out from there to include faith in the unseen reality. It all depends on 'evidence': what evidence have we got that the symbol in the middle: the teacher, the authority, the message, the book, is reliable? If we have evidence that the teacher is reliable, then we have <u>faith</u> in the teacher (the symbol), and we know for sure 'that America exists' when he tells us so, even if we can't see the land. And all this is the same for any 'scientist' a million times a day, even when he is trying to tell you that he is a rationalist, and that he has no faith! He is 'rationalist' enough to have faith in his books and papers, his teachers, his peers, his instruments, his friends and even his bank account ...

We have collected enough information to come straight to the point. In everyday life, if the 'symbol' (the teacher, the authority, the wording of a message, the instrument, the guide or whatever medium) is accepted: 'believed', the mind comes in contact with the unseen 'thing'. If the symbol is rejected, the mind does not come in contact with the unseen 'thing'. It depends on individual cases if the unseen 'thing' becomes an unseen reality.

Believing the symbol is coming to the knowledge of the unseen 'thing' it mediates. If a teacher tells the children 'that the earth is flat', and he is believed, then the minds of the children 'have come in contact' with the idea of a flat earth, a 'thing' even if this is not reality.

Not believing the symbol is rejecting the knowledge of the unseen 'thing', even if the thing is a true reality.

If a truth relationship exists between the symbol and the unseen 'thing', (i.e. if what the symbol conveys is correct, which could merely be a few 'words' on a slip of paper: "You have won Tatts lotto!"), then the mind's knowledge has become knowledge of an unseen reality, and this knowledge is true if the symbol is believed. The mind is in error if the symbol is not believed. In that case ignorance of the unseen reality cannot be truthfully claimed. Like the pilot in our first example above: if he survives after rejecting the true information supplied to him by his instruments, he cannot, at his trial, claim ignorance of the true knowledge of the unseen realities he had received.

If there is a relationship of error between the symbol and the unseen 'thing' it veils, then the mind is in error if the symbol is believed. The mind is guarded from error (but not necessarily in possession of the truth), if in this case the symbol is rejected. If, in the above example, some children do not believe the teacher telling them the earth is flat, then their minds are closed for the idea of a flat earth and they are guarded against error in not believing in a flat earth, and believing in its direct opposite: "The earth is not flat". They are thereby not necessarily in the possession of the truth 'that the earth is approximately a sphere'.

Turning now to a text in Sacred Scripture, the famous 'definition of faith' in the Letter to the Hebrews, Ch. 11, v. 1, we can from the various translations given to this text clearly gather the truth of what has been said so far. Here are four translations:

Vulgate (Douay):	"Now faith is the substance of things to be hoped for, the evidence of things that appear not."

Knox:	"Faith is that which gives substance to our hopes; which convinces us of things we cannot see."
Jerusalem:	"Only faith can guarantee the blessings we hope for, or prove the existence of realities that at present remain unseen."
RSV:	"Now faith is the assurance of things hoped for, the conviction of things not seen."

The first thing that strikes us as common in all these various translations is that the ancient author of the text must have considered faith to be an intellectual act. Words such as 'evidence', 'convinces', 'prove', 'conviction' do not leave room for any other conclusion. 'I believe' is therefore considered by the Holy Spirit, the true Author of Sacred Scripture, to be a submission of a mind 'convinced' on 'evidence' of a 'proven truth'. This is entirely in conformity with our everyday experiences as set out above.

Furthermore, all the translations quoted here stress the fact that the act of faith is about 'unseen realities'.

And finally, if we are allowed to adduce here another famous text of St. Paul on faith: "Fides ex auditu", "faith comes from hearing", then we can complete our comparison of this scriptural definition with what went before, by pointing out that the normal 'symbol' of faith is 'words': words spoken or written with authority.

If we now read in the Jerusalem bible that this definition of faith in Hebrews 11:1 must be considered as a theological definition of Faith with-a-capital-F, that is an accurate description of an act of the Supernatural, infused, Divine Gift of Faith, then we see from our comparison, that our basic and true understanding of faith will not suffer any violence if it is raised to an understanding that is inspired by Revelation. Another example of a human truth "chiming in, by a pre-established harmony, with Divine Revelation". [Pope Pius XII in *Humani Generis,* 1950]

Because of this 'chiming in', Supernatural Faith must now also be seen as 'a-way-of-knowing', but one to which our human nature with its unaided intellect is altogether incapable. The gift of Faith requires two things: an additional supernatural faculty to properly perform acts of Faith, as well as an additional supernatural Light to 'see' by, to allow the human being to see the Revealed Truths in the supernatural Light of that new faculty. The seat for this new faculty with its new, additional Light is in the ordinary human intellect. Christ makes it abundantly clear in the Gospel that, once this new power to believe Revealed Truths, this faculty and this Light, has been given to a human being, He expects <u>us</u> to be responsible for its operation with the aid of God's grace, in order that it can be truly <u>meritorious</u>.

The classic example of this dual aspect of the one act of Faith, is Peter's famous 'Profession of Faith' Mt. 16:16, and Our Lord's confirmation in the very next verse, v. 17.

> "'But you', He said, 'who do you say I am?' Then Simon Peter spoke up 'You are the Christ', he said, 'the Son of the Living God'.

> Jesus replied, 'Simon, son of John, you are a blessed man. Because it was not flesh and blood that revealed this to you, but My Father in heaven. So now I say to you: You are Peter, and on this Rock I will build My Church'..." [Mt. 16: 15-18].

Peter attested here to a truth, which, according to the words of the Creator of the human intellect, he could not possibly have arrived at by his own natural powers; but had been revealed to him from above. Yet, it was <u>Peter's</u> profession of Faith. And just as Our Lady had been called 'blessed' for grasping and believing what had come to Her from above by the message of an Angel, and just as Christ called Peter 'blessed' for believing and professing what had been revealed to him by the Father, that is, for performing his very own meritorious Act of Faith, so others will, in the end, be held personally responsible for <u>not</u> believing: for refusing to use that supernatural faculty by <u>not</u> making a profession of Faith …

"But he that believeth not shall be condemned."

[Mk. I6: 16.]

We do well therefore never to separate Mt. 16:16 from Mk 16:16.

The supernatural gift of Faith still has the three essentials we discovered to be part of an ordinary act of human faith:

- it too is about unseen realities, which are guaranteed to be true Supernatural Realities by divine Authority;
- it too centres on symbols: Words and divine Authority, by which these true realities are veiled, but through which we are in touch with them once Faith in the symbols is professed;
- it too is seated in the human intellect, ever searching for its proper object: truth.

The only difference is that the human intellect receives from God the necessary power to perform these acts of Faith, surpassing mere human power: a supernatural faculty and a supernatural Light, both of which will, like any other human faculty, grow stronger through repeated use.

Before we finally can settle the question 'Which Faith-with-a-capital-F is pleasing to God?', we must have a closer look at the environment in which so many of the acts of human faith are formally made: the teaching situation.

We can truthfully say that all teaching plays its role as the trusted 'symbol' in that sacred 'no-man's land' between the enquiring mind and the unseen but sought-after realities. And here teaching fulfils a triple purpose:

(i) it creates a situation where mind and symbol can meet for the possession of the unseen realities;

(ii) it gathers evidence for the inquiring mind to induce it to give its assent (the act of faith in the teacher) in order to reach the truth and the good that this knowledge brings with it;

(iii) it incorporates the already mentioned 'symbol of authority' to facilitate the transition from 'enquiring' to 'assent'.

Here we see emerge the glaring deficiencies of the Modernists as teachers. They refuse to treat the 'no-man's land' as sacred and they refuse to create the situation mentioned in (i), preferring instead to work by stealth and deception. They reject the necessity for evidence for their gravely erroneous doctrines, preferring the use of coercion. They constantly try to stifle opposition, browbeating ordinary folk into simply accepting their 'authority' on their own recommendation, or else be savaged by them!

It is an established Dogma of the Catholic Church that Our Lord made it a pre-requisite of the REDEMPTIVE power of the true Faith, that His Authority would always be present in that 'no-man's land', and that this Authority would be vested in the Papacy. In other words, the teaching authority of the Catholic Church has the right and duty to be present between the believer and the Article of Faith held up to be believed (the Symbol of Faith) in order that the unseen Realities of God's Revealed Truths can come into the believing mind, and heart and life. And this teaching authority is vested primarily in the Pope, and only through the Papacy is it also vested in the College of Bishops united with the Pope by an untrammeled Catholic Faith.

Here it becomes clear which Faith must be pleasing to God: the act of the Supernatural, Infused, Divine and <u>Catholic</u> Faith, and why this is so. And when we become aware, that Catholic Faith must be essentially different from any other faith, as only <u>one</u> Faith can be pleasing to God in its own right, then it is not hard for us to complete the picture by realising that it must be possible to make this difference crystal clear. For we accept that here, at last, we have come to the bedrock spoken of in the first page of this chapter. Only One Faith demands that the Christ-appointed teaching authority be permanently present between the believing minds and the unseen, Revealed Realities to be believed. And the Church that professes that ONE, unique Faith, and provides us with the mechanics of this unique mediation, must of necessity be the ONE True Church!

Is it not a tragedy that humanity not only accepts but demands the mediation of a good teacher, a trustworthy authority, a reliable instrument between itself and the faith that leads to certain knowledge, yet rejects the Authority of a God-appointed mediation in the most critical and vital Faith we have on this planet: Faith that leads everyone to eternal salvation, into the actual presence of the 'unseen Realities' spoken of in the Letter to the Hebrews [11:1]?

Let us follow the contours of the Church built on the bedrock of this claim, and see how She Herself, and the Faith within Her, differ from any other church or faith, and on Whose Authority. To obtain maximum benefit, we will begin this final section of our preliminary investigations by contrasting Catholic Faith against its nearest rival, the Protestant christian faith, before letting the Holy Spirit give the final verdict.

The long lapse of some four hundred and fifty years may have obscured somewhat the vehemence with which the Protestant Reformation set about its business in Europe and England. And the decline of Protestantism, reduced to a 'spent force' in spiritual political matters two centuries later, did not go unnoticed amongst writers of repute. Writing about the rise of Freemasonry and atheism in the middle of the eighteenth century, Mgr. George F. Dillon,

DD, has this to say in his literary classic *The War of Antichrist with the Church and Christian Civilization* (1885):

> "The so-called Reformation, which arose and continued to progress during the two preceding centuries, had well nigh run its course. The principle of private judgement, introduced in apparent zeal for the pure worship and doctrines of Christ, had ended in leaving no part of the teaching of Christ unchallenged. It had rendered His Divinity disbelieved, and His very existence doubted by many who called themselves His followers ..."

"The principle of private judgement ..."

If that was the corner stone of the Protestant revolt (and who is there to deny it) then it is precisely here that we touch on the 'bedrock' where Catholicism and Protestantism differ fundamentally in faith and structure. Protestantism claiming that Christ did not put any mediator between Himself and the believer willing to give his assent in faith, whilst the Catholic Church maintains that She received authority from Christ Himself to teach:

(i) to what symbols assent must be given in Catholic Faith in order to reach Supernatural Reality: Truth, Life in God, Salvation; and
(ii) from what symbols assent must be withheld as <u>not</u> reaching Supernatural Reality and Truth, and so no Life in God and Salvation.

The Protestant Revolt could never have ended up in a 'true Church', as the nature of a revolt is to object to the existence of something that was there prior to the revolt, and do away with it. Even Protestants will admit that prior to their revolt the True Church of Christ may have existed, having possessed for centuries beforehand the very thing they revolted against! If this True Church did not continue to exist in their persuasion after the revolt, as their 'church' no longer possessed what the True Church before them had enjoyed for centuries, then the True Church must have continued alongside them and independently from them, because it is unthinkable that Christ would not stand by the True Church He had founded.

The Catholic Church has always claimed that Christ left on earth a teaching authority in the Church He founded, to decide in His Name what to believe and what not to believe. And the Faith that believes that and submits to it is the Holy Catholic Faith in the Holy Catholic Church. Making this Faith and this Church not only different from any other 'faith' or 'church', but also unique!

And now for some evidence for this.

We have finally found our way into the presence of 'the pearl of great beauty' for the possession of which millions upon millions of human beings have been prepared, are still prepared and will continue to be prepared to sacrifice everything in order either to keep it or gain it: Catholic Faith, THE most precious Gift, according to the Doctors of the Church and all the Saints, of Almighty God to man.

"Faith without which it is impossible to please God." [Hebr. 11:6], says the holy author of the Letter to the Hebrews, before launching into the most magnificent exaltation of Faith, world literature has ever known, since it was inspired by God Himself. Where then do we begin our final analysis? We begin where Christ Himself began.

Calling sinners to a personal salvation through repentance, forgiveness and holiness of life, in obedience to the teachings of the Church He founded, is still the central core of Jesus' Mission and Message today. It is also still the central message from Heaven. "STOP SINNING" was the very first injunction from Our Blessed Lady at Fatima to the whole world, when She revealed Herself as 'Our Lady of the Rosary' during Her final apparition on OCT 13, 1917.

According to the Will of Our Saviour, and according to the solemn teaching of the Church He founded, this personal salvation has a distinct beginning. It's 'initium': beginning, 'radix': root, and 'fundamentum': foundation is the Act of Supernatural, Infused, Divine and Catholic Faith. The Catholic Church's teaching on this is quite clear and specific. In its Fifth Session, the Council of Trent has laid down as Catholic Doctrine how the above-quoted text in Hebr. 11:6 is to be understood for all times. Referring to this text directly, it says:

> "It is our Catholic Faith without which it is impossible to please God." [Denz. Schm. 1510].

And again in its Sixth Session, elaborating on this most important doctrine, the Council of Trent continued:

> "When the Apostle tells us that man is justified by Faith, and freely so, then these words must be understood in the sense that the Catholic Church has held and expressed this with perpetual unanimity, namely that we are justified by Faith, because Faith is the beginning of the salvation of man, and the foundation and root of all justification and without which it is impossible to please God", quoting again the same text from Hebr. 11:6.

With its repeated referral to this text in Hebrews 11, and after having previously taught us with Christ's authority, that 'faith' in this text is to be understood as 'Catholic Faith', the Council now proceeds to give the explanation of its own teaching when it said:

> "... these words must be understood in the sense that the Catholic Church has held and expressed this with perpetual unanimity ..."

And what was it that the Council of Trent taught the Universal Church in its Fifth Session? That 'Faith' in this text must be understood as 'Catholic Faith'. If that is what the Church 'has held and expressed with perpetual unanimity', then the Council is now declaring with the authority of Christ that it remains Catholic Faith 'which is the beginning, the foundation and the root of all justification'. Even if before the Protestant revolt, this was to be taken as synonymous with 'Christian Faith', the Council here and now makes crystal clear that the Catholic position 'held and expressed with perpetual unanimity': that, if from now on, 'christian faith' is held up in opposition to Catholic Faith, then it may no longer be accepted as the 'beginning, root, and foundation of ALL justification'.

In her Dogmatic Constitution 'Dei Filius', "De Fide Catholica": "On Catholic Faith", the First Vatican Council took over the same teaching, the same quotes, and confirmed that the same interpretation must be given to Catholic Faith. It then took the matter further.

What is the significance of all this?

For one, it means that after the Council of Trent there is now a distinct difference the 'freedom' of 'somehow believing in whatever' the Protestant 'christian' way, and 'believing in whatever' the way the Holy Catholic Church stipulates Catholics must believe. It does <u>not</u> mean that only 'Catholics go to heaven' and that Protestants will not go to heaven unless they believe with Catholic Faith. But it does mean that Catholic Faith, the Faith professed in humility and obedience to the Catholic Church, is so pleasing to God, that He made it 'the beginning, root and foundation, of everybody else's justification'. It means that no other faith on its own saves the believer, but if the other believer will be saved, he or she will have to thank the Catholic Church, and the unique Catholic Faith within Her, for the necessary graces. If it is true that Catholic Faith is 'the beginning, the root and foundation of ALL justification, then the Catholic Church and the Catholic Faith within Her have been made by Christ ABSOLUTELY NECESSARY for salvation here on earth, anyone's salvation, including those not professing the Catholic Faith.

It finally means that a heavy obligation has been laid on the shoulders of all those who freely received from God this priceless light and power, to keep it at all cost! It is truly God's greatest gift, because only in that Supernatural Light can we see with the eyes of Faith all the Holy Realities God has given us: His Son, His Holy Mother, His presence in the Blessed Eucharist, His Church, the pearls of His teaching, His Face in the poor, the true meaning of the Scriptures, and His Truth in *Humanae Vitae* ... And only in Catholic Faith lies the foundation of Hope: Hebrews 11:1.

Chapter Five

Conscience in the Light of Catholic Faith

On a few occasions in this narrative I had reason to quote the words with which Pope Pius XII lauded the 'Philosophia Perennis' of St. Thomas Aquinas, that most magnificent and realistic 'thought-system' at the root of Catholic theology:

> "His teaching appears to chime in, by a kind of pre-established harmony, with Divine Revelation."

How uncanny this papal observation is that, when the principles of this philosophy are used for the acquisition of accurate understanding of things in everyday life, we can then see how the truths thus acquired chime in with what we know is true from Divine Revelation. This can be appreciated from a little experiment, which it is good to do here for the round-up of the difficult subject-matter of the previous chapter. Apart from reinforcing some of the important aspects of what went before, this short resume will also suit the purpose of introducing the subject-matter which has been selected as the topic for this chapter: the relationship between Faith and conscience.

I refer the reader to a short passage I wrote in the previous chapter. To facilitate comparison it is repeated here for your convenience.

> "In <u>all</u> these cases, it is the reliability of 'the symbol in the middle', which induces faith in the symbol itself, stretching out from there to include faith in the unseen reality. It all depends on 'evidence': what evidence have we got that the symbol in the middle: the teacher, the authority, the message, the book, is reliable? If we have evidence that the teacher is reliable, then we have <u>faith</u> in the teacher (the symbol), and we know for sure 'that America exists' when he tells us so, even if we can't see the land."

We do not have to change much to make the truth of this passage 'chime in' with what we know is true from Revelation:

> "In the case of the Catholic Faith, it is the reliability of 'the symbol in the middle', the Catholic Church, which induces Faith in the Church Herself, stretching out from there to include Faith in the Unseen Realities. It all depends on evidence: what evidence have we got that the 'symbol in the middle': the Church's Magisterium, Her Authority, the Gospel Message, the Bible, are reliable? If we have evidence that the teaching Church is reliable, then we have Faith in the Church, the Symbol of Faith, and we <u>know</u> for sure 'that Heaven exists' when She tells us so, even if we can't see the 'Promised Land'."

From the simple fact that these two examples bear comparison we conclude that a human truth, ascertainable by proper thought-processes, (example one) will not cease to be a truth in the supernatural order (when compared with example two) but will be upheld in total harmony with <u>all</u> creation 'for the greater glory of God'.

In both cases (we said) "it all hinges on evidence: evidence that 'the symbol in the middle': the teacher, Church, is reliable". It is outside the scope of this little work to adduce all the compelling reasons from 'Apologetics' to prove beyond doubt that the reliability of the Catholic Church, as the God-appointed 'Symbol of Faith in the middle', is a Revealed Truth, and so is divinely guaranteed. For the preservation of <u>Catholic</u> Faith in <u>all</u> Revelation, assent to this Dogma of the absolute reliability of the Catholic Church must be given first by every Catholic, before contact in Faith with the Unseen Realities beyond can be made. But what I can do by way of a most effective 'short-cut' is, to show how yet another truth from sound philosophy 'chimes in' with what we know to be true from Revelation. The comparison above shows that this is a valid exercise.

From Catholic Philosophy we know how intimately connected to human nature 'private ownership' is. We still ought to be vividly aware, especially in the centenary year of *Rerum Novarum* after 70 years of Communism, how Pope Leo XIII has made this human right inviolable. And in the third chapter of this little book, we have come to understand how, even in judging the 'tree' in a man's heart, we must be careful not to judge the owner, even if he is the owner of a whole diseased orchard. We can only judge the use he makes of it from his own words, and from the effect he has on others.

From the same reliable source, we know that St. Thomas, unlike most philosophers after him, does not place the essence of 'personhood' in 'self-awareness' but in 'self-possession'. A person, according to St. Thomas, is someone who possesses himself / herself. And the fullness of bliss in Heaven, according to this same reliable teaching, does not so much lie in the 'vision' of God as in the 'possession' of Him! These truths must now be seen to 'chime in' with what we know from Revelation and the infinite mercy of God.

Like any other prudently given faith, Catholic Faith too arrives at true knowledge. Knowledge of God and the Blessed Trinity, and all of the other Supernatural Realities God has revealed to us. And the Catholic Church was indeed founded by Christ as the guarantor of absolute accuracy in the handing down and the preservation of this knowledge, this 'vision' in the Light of Faith. But since securing true knowledge is all ordinary faith and a reliable 'symbol' (teacher) are able to do, then it is here where all similarities between ordinary faith and Catholic Faith, and between a human mediator (teacher) and the Catholic Church come to an end. For, by the mercy of God, Catholic Faith is able to do more, infinitely more than handing down Supernatural knowledge.

The Father, knowing, as the Creator of the human heart, how important 'possession' is for us, His children, not only wanted us to <u>know</u> Him in Catholic Faith, but to possess Him, already here on earth. Children who accept in faith their favourite teacher's declaration that 'America exists' can only go so far: they possess true knowledge, but they do not possess America! But in Catholic Faith it is not only the knowledge, however accurate, of the Unseen Realities, that counts but their possession. 'My' God. 'My' Mother Mary. 'My' Holy Mother the Catholic Church. 'My' Sacred Heart. 'My' Holy Communion. 'My' forgiveness. The vows of 'my' Baptism. 'My' personal Guardian Angel. The Communion of Saints is 'my' home.

It was for the safeguarding of this possession, this intimacy, far beyond mere knowledge, that only an absolute certainty could be attached by Christ to the Gift of Catholic Faith in the Catholic Church. A certainty that is absolute to such an extent that, if it is doubted, the Faith itself is doubted, and the priceless Gift is in danger of being lost. And with the loss of Faith in the Catholic Church Herself comes the loss of the invaluable possession of this intimacy with (and not only the knowledge of) the unseen Realities beyond! Thus when the Father wanted us to have this intimacy, this <u>possession</u> of 'Things Unseen' in Catholic Faith, He attached, by His Divine Veracity, absolute certainty to the one and only Act that immediately mediates this intimate possession: the act of Supernatural, Infused and Divine Faith IN THE CATHOLIC CHURCH His Son founded on the man he called 'blessed' to head that Church!

For Catholics, the worry is not the loss of Faith in any of the unseen Realities: this is only a sign of a greater and much earlier loss: the loss of Catholic Faith in the Catholic Church Herself! And with <u>that</u>

loss a Catholic loses not only intellectual contact with the one unseen Reality he lost Faith in, but the possession of all unseen Realities: Christ, Mary, Confession, the Blessed Eucharist, etc. For the foundation of Catholic Faith in the divinity of Christ, is not some unrelated 'christian faith', but the priceless Gift of Catholic Faith in the God-appointed Mediator between man and all unseen Realities. If Faith in this one divinely appointed mediator (the Catholic Church) is lost in regard to only one Revealed Truth, Faith in the Catholic Church itself is lost. And with the single loss of Faith in this one supernatural Reality, the Catholic Church, access to the intimate knowledge needed for possession of all Revealed Truths is forever blocked. Loss of Faith in only one Revealed Truth taught by the Catholic Church shows loss of Faith in the Catholic Church itself. And it is this loss which bars forever access to what lies beyond.

In 1910 this loss of Faith was so widespread that Pope St. Pius X wrote of "the great movement of apostasy organised in every country for the establishment of a One-World 'Church'".

Every Pope as the Vicar of Christ on earth, has received from above the authority to make known 'what is in the Mind of Christ'. The historical fact, then, that this Pope and Saint, under Divine guidance, could predict with certainty the formation of a counter-'church' as the instrument of God's punishment for the apostasy, shows clearly that, 'in the Mind of Christ', the essence of apostasy is not the loss of Catholic Faith in a particular Dogma, but the loss of Faith in the Catholic Church teaching this particular Dogma! The enforced mass entry into a 'Church of Darkness' shows God's wrath over massive desertions from the One True Church of Light.

We may now better understand the expression: 'Catholic Faith, the greatest gift of God to man'. There are greater Unseen Realities but their possession depends entirely, yes even exclusively, on the possession of this Faith: Faith in the Catholic Church and in all that the Catholic Church proposes for Belief. A priest who no longer believes that the Holy Spirit proceeds from the Father and the Son, not only loses the 'possession' (indwelling) of the Holy Spirit: he loses the possession of Everything, as he has truly lost the greatest Gift: his Faith in the Catholic Church teaching him how to believe the Dogma of the Blessed Trinity.

One more question about Catholic Faith must be settled, before Conscience can be seen in the totality of the only Light that matters: "How permanent is the loss of Catholic Faith?"

The answer from Holy Scripture is frightening! So indeed is its echo in History. To say nothing of the groans in Hell ...

Only one Faith has been given to humanity, which is meritorious and life-giving in its own right, as only one Faith can be "the beginning, the root and the foundation of ALL justification". It is the Faith in the unique Church that came forth from the pierced Heart of the Redeemer on the Cross, His very own Mystical Body and Bride, Our Holy Mother the Catholic Church. It is Faith in the only Church of which 'blessed Peter' has been made the Rock, and over which each successor of Peter has the authority of Christ as His Vicar on earth. It is that sole priceless possession, on which the salvation of everyone depends, as no other faith under heaven leads to salvation in its own right and name.

If that were possible, then apostasy from the Catholic Faith and transition to 'that other faith' would not constitute THE most serious mortal sin, as in God's eyes, it would merely be a simple transition from one life-giving Faith to another. This is impossible for two reasons.

(i) Since we are dealing here with a non-Catholic faith, then the obvious fact about this faith would be that it is <u>outside</u> the Catholic Church. Were God to give life-giving powers to this faith in its own right, then He would teach through the Catholic Church with His Divine Veracity that "outside the Catholic Church there are no means of salvation" ['*Extra Ecclesiam nulla salus*'], at the same time that He would be teaching outside the Catholic Church (through that other faith) 'that outside the Catholic Church there is at least one other means of salvation', this other 'faith', which directly negates the first proposition and is of course an impossible contradiction. The single mindedness of a pure contradiction demands that both propositions can neither be both true nor can they be both false. This means that, if one is true, the other MUST be false, and vice versa. Were a non-Catholic faith a truly life-giving faith, then EVERYTHING in the Catholic Church that flows directly from Her fundamental claim, including the Faith therein, must be a lie, a falsehood and a fraud.

(ii) A second essential feature of this non-Catholic faith would be that, being by definition the negation of the Catholic Faith (non Catholic), it is its immediate contradiction. The negation of a truth cannot itself be true. If a non-Catholic faith by definition denies the truths of the Catholic Faith, then it is a false faith and cannot claim to have God on side to make it life-giving in its own right. Since this is essentially the same situation as in (i) above, a Catholic cannot adhere part-

> ly to the Catholic Faith and partly to a non-Catholic faith at the same time (as seems to be a widespread custom nowadays) since Catholic Faith and its direct negation, non Catholic, cannot be both true at the same time. One cannot pick and choose what to believe and what not to believe in the Catholic Church, as Faith in the Catholic Church Herself is all-inclusive, and precedes Faith in any of Her Dogmas.

The Holy Catholic Church has expressed this most beautifully in one of the Second Vatican Council's documents, the one on Divine Revelation, *Dei Verbum*:

> "But the task of giving an authentic interpretation of the Word of God, whether in its written form or in the form of Tradition, has been entrusted to the living teaching office of the Church alone ... It is clear therefore that in the supremely wise arrangement of God, sacred Tradition, sacred Scripture and

> the Magisterium of the Church are so connected and associated, that one of them cannot stand without the others." [#10].

In other words, loss of Catholic Faith in any part of the Catholic Church's teachings ends up in loss of Faith in all Her teachings ('one of them cannot stand without the others'), because disbelieving only one aspect reveals a previous loss of Faith in the Church Herself!

The enormity of the evil of apostasy, and the reason why the Holy Catholic Faith is called a priceless possession, are only truly understood if it is realised through the loss of this invaluable gift of Faith, Catholics not only lose some intellectual knowledge of God and His Revealed Treasures, but as we saw THEIR POSSESSION! And the evil of its loss is compounded if it is further realised, that the Gift was freely given to us for the benefit of others. Which means that the loss of Catholic Faith ensures that non-Catholics, originally by God's Providence entrusted to the Catholic Faith of apostates, are in great danger of missing out on the graces needed for their eternal salvation and their own share in this possession, unless heroic victim souls in the Mystical Body of Christ are prepared to take over this duty of passing on the Faith and its life-giving graces, interrupted by the apostasy of fellow Catholics.

Apostasy, the terrifying loss of the possession of God, which had been freely given with the Gift of Catholic Faith. Who or what can restore the uprooted Gift, the only means to gain back the rejected possession? If, with the Light of Faith, the knowledge and the possession of God were not considered valuable enough to possess, how can blindness and utter darkness be expected to restore now, what could not be seen with the help of the eyes of Faith in the Supernatural Light? Beside, since the gift of true Faith was God's gift, no human being can restore it. No human being can pay for it, since it is a free gift. Only a miracle of grace can restore it, and God is not required to perform a miracle. The only hope for an apostate is the supernatural love of loved ones who, as true victim souls in the Mystical Body of Christ, are prepared through prayer and suffering to sacrifice themselves, in order to obtain from God the ultimate in love: the miracle of grace needed for the restoration of the lost Faith.

This is a very serious matter. The 'beginning, root and foundation of Justification' will only be given once. Any other lapse or mishap can be forgiven because, in the Light of Faith, we can see the enormity of sin, and we can ask for forgiveness, seeing in the same Light, the Revealed Reality of God's Mercy. But what, if the light had been extinguished after it had been given, and Catholic Faith is killed? Not just kept dormant or inoperative by indifference and by a life of debauchery and sin as is so often the case, but given up, exchanged? When the possession of God and His treasures has been exchanged for the possession of mere creatures? With the gift of Catholic Faith, God gave the recipients a priceless possession. If the consequences for keeping it are enormous for the salvation of the human race, so are the repercussions for abandoning it ...

Sacred Scripture is adamant about the impossibility of forgiveness after apostasy in the ordinary economy of Grace. The text that follows here, taken from St. Paul's Letter to the Hebrews is headed in the Jerusalem bible with this remark: 'The danger of apostasy'.

"If, after we have been given knowledge of the Truth, we should deliberately commit any sins (against this Light that is) then there is no longer any sacrifice for them. There will be left only the dreadful prospect of Judgement and of the raging fire that is to burn rebels. Anyone who disregards the Law of Moses is ruthlessly put to death on the word of two witnesses or three; and you maybe sure that anyone who tramples on the Son of God and who treats the Blood of the Covenant which sanctified him as if it were unholy and who insults the Spirit of Grace, will be condemned to a far severer punishment. We are all well aware Who it was that said 'Vengeance is mine, I will repay'. And again 'The Lord will judge His people'. It is a dreadful thing to fall into the hands of the living God ...

'The righteous man will live by Faith, but if he draws back, My soul will take no pleasure in Him'.

We are not the children of withdrawing unto perdition, but of Faith for the salvation of our souls."

[Hebrews. 10:26-31; 38-39].

If someone, having come this far, would be inclined to think, that I took my time coming to the second topic of this chapter, Conscience, then I hope that there are plenty 'out there' capable of setting this person's mind at rest by realising themselves, that (i) nothing can be viewed in the Light of Faith until Faith itself has been completely illuminated by that Light, and (ii) that indeed I have been saying plenty already about Catholic conscience, without so much as mentioning the word. For it is true that the conscience of a true child of the Holy Church will always make decisions which are completely Catholic. Or at least ought to make such decisions, and is expected to make them. This tells us that, with Catholics, the stronger Light of Faith guides the much more uncertain light of conscience, which shows that a good understanding of Catholic Faith has a direct bearing on a Catholic's conscience decisions. For Catholics it is much safer and a lot closer to the truth to say 'My Faith does not allow me to do this or that' than to say 'My conscience does not allow me to do this or that'. For if a Catholic's conscience is held up or invoked AGAINST the Faith, he or she may end up as Luther who is reported to have said: 'In conscience here I stand. I cannot go back'. By then he had lost his Catholic Faith, so his appeal to 'conscience' was grandstanding and totally useless, as the above quoted text from Sacred Scripture reveals. All the foregoing was therefore needed to eventually impress on Catholics that the Holy Church demands that a Catholic's conscience be informed.

[1] Even for a good appreciation of the role of conscience in non-Catholics, the understanding of Catholic Faith is a must. We know that Catholic Faith is essential for the 'justification' of all. That means that Faith in the Catholic Church, and all the good works performed in the Light of that Faith, constantly release the fullness of Grace inside the Church from Her Head Jesus Christ to flow out to every person on earth. And since the origin of this

---

[1] This is the beginning of the section referred to in footnote 5, in the 'Note' at the end of this book.

Grace is from true Faith: from the Faith of Catholics in the Catholic Church, the Faith that justifies, the first urge of that Grace is always 'to justify' the recipients, that is, to get them into the state of Sanctifying Grace, like Abraham was justified (sanctified) by true Faith.

Now it is important to quote here once again what the Second Vatican Council taught us about this, which quote appears in the Foreword of this book.

> "Nevertheless many elements of sanctification and of truth are found outside its visible confines. Since (i) these are gifts properly belonging to the Church of Christ, (ii) they are forces impelling to Catholic unity."

The Graces 'of sanctification and truth' that flow out of the Catholic Church (i) bear the stamp of their Catholic origin, and remain the possession of that Church; and (ii) BECAUSE OF THAT ORIGIN impress themselves on the conscience of every recipient as 'a force impelling to Catholic unity', which is first and foremost a 'unity in Faith'. So, it is

Church doctrine that not only Catholic consciences must be consciences 'informed by Catholic Faith', but that ALL consciences are constantly under that blessed, dynamic influence. Why? Because God wants every human being not only to come to the knowledge of Him, but also to POSSESS Him already here on earth! And the source of the true knowledge and of the true possession is vested in Catholic Faith. (Now think back on the evil of apostasy in the Light of <u>this</u> teaching!).

This is what I meant when I wrote that the Light of Catholic Faith, a Light that has its origin in Eternity, is needed to get a proper appreciation of 'conscience'. We will give the reader shortly the additional information on conscience from Catholic Philosophy 'which chimes in, as by a kind of pre-established harmony, with Divine Revelation'. But already here the sacred Council teaches that conscience must be viewed as a kind of 'divine bridgehead' in individuals for God to get His supernatural treasures across, flowing out from the One True Church His Son founded for that very purpose. And it is obvious that the Holy Catholic Church expects Catholics not only to make full use of that 'bridgehead', but to depend on it in the work of salvation. And once again we will be able to marvel at the precision with which 'the human carillon' on the teachings of the human conscience chimes in with 'the supernatural carillon': the role of conscience in the teachings of Revealed Truth as explained by Church teaching on Faith, Grace and Conscience.

So far we have seen God's action in the salvation of souls. How He works exclusively through the Catholic Church in which the fullness of grace is found because only this Holy Church is connected to Her Head Jesus Christ in which "the fullness of grace" [Jo. 1:16] and the "fullness of the Godhead" dwell. [Col. 2:9]. Moreover, it is only in the Catholic Church alone, in the Blessed Sacrament, where this fullness of grace and Godhead is bodily abiding, made present on Her altars by Catholic Faith. This shows overwhelmingly that these graces 'bear the stamp of their origin' and must be truly referred to as Catholic graces. If received well by non-Catholics in the 'divine bridgehead' (their human conscience open to Grace), they will produce the first stirrings towards full Catholic unity in Faith, so that a more complete possession of God and His supernatural treasures can be enjoyed as far as this is possible on earth. From then on Grace can begin to flow out to others from the Catholic Faith in this new Catholic life. Trained theologians reading this will understand that the Council is talking here about what St. Thomas calls the '*fides inchoata*' in the human soul, the first awakening to, the subsequent longing for, and the beginning of positive cooperation with the divine invitation to accept the Gift of Faith.

What is still left over for us to do is to investigate how all this works on the human side. What are, to use a popular phrase, the 'mechanics' of this interaction? What is this conscience, and how does it become a kind of 'divine bridgehead' under the imperceptible influence of grace? Here, as already promised we would do, we can only turn to one thought-system which alone bears the stamp of the Church's approval, having been singled out as chiming in with the workings of grace and Redemption as revealed to us by divine Revelation. Since conscience is not a supernatural Light but a human light, proper to human nature, Catholic Philosophy will discover it and can pronounce on it.

(I must stress that here only theoretical principles from a trustworthy Philosophy can be given. How the endless combinations of psychological, moral and intellectual influences interfere with the basic pattern differs from person to person, and must be studied and taken into consideration in individual counselling. But experts in these fields would be wasting their time if they ignored, or were ignorant of, the true foundations of the interaction between Grace and Conscience as discovered in the only Philosophy which carries the guarantee that it has this interaction right. This is the same as saying that only Thomism can tell us how this interaction should work according to the <u>one</u> reliable 'blueprint' which the Creator has made to underlie <u>all</u> personal differences: the <u>one</u> human nature. As we know from papal assurances, the Holy Church is confident that Thomism found the 'key' needed for the accurate reading of this blueprint.)[2]

Creation then, according to Church belief, is the calling into existence by the Almighty of other beings outside Himself, who will be forever stamped

---

[2] This is the end of the section referred to in footnote 5, in the 'Note' at the end of this book.

with at least two characteristics concerning their origin:

(i) '*ab initio*': with a beginning, and
(ii) '*ex nihilo*': from nothing.

Since we speak about 'the Act of Creation', St. Thomas found it very convenient to keep alive in his system this powerful meaning of 'this first act' of the Almighty, and to keep the term 'act' connected to this whole idea of 'calling into being' or 'being called into being'. From here on we will restrict ourselves deliberately to the crown and glory of the material creation: the human being. From (i) above we see that the human being 'exists', albeit with a limited existence, and from (ii) above we accept that we can truthfully say of the human being that, surrounding his limited existence, 'there is a lot he is NOT'...

Since the human being cannot give himself his own existence, his existence depends so much on 'the first act of creation', that St. Thomas calls 'existence' by its proper name: '*actus primus*', 'first or primary act'. My existence as a human being is 'the first act' or 'the primary act' about me, but not my first or primary act since I did not make myself. I was called into being by Someone else's 'primary act'. Once created as a human being by this 'primary act', I am now a living 'primary act': His primary act as far as my existence is concerned. However, once constituted in existence as a 'primary act', I am now able to perform my own acts, that is, as we saw, I can 'call into being' what was not. All these acts, my acts, St. Thomas calls 'secondary acts', '*actus secundus*'. It is clear that my secondary acts flow totally and only from the nature the Creator called into being when He gave me existence, when He gave me my personal 'primary act', my existence. My secondary acts are limited by the nature I received in the primary act.

Now it is very necessary that we come to terms with that sea of 'not-my-existence' surrounding every human being, that immense expanse of all that the human being is not, but (according to (ii) above, and this remains important) from which he came. If his 'primary act', his own existence, came from what is not, then it is the fate of all his (own) secondary acts, that they share in this fate, and that they too come from what was not before. Even the simple task of putting my hand to my head shows the difference between primary and secondary act. My hand is part of 'my primary act', my human existence. It is there, but it was not always there. It too was created and came from nothing. But when I put my hand to my head, my secondary act, I must admit that it was Not there a minute ago and that I could have put it somewhere else. All my secondary acts, that is all that I now bring into existence, remain surrounded by a vast expanse of what I COULD have done, a sea of 'possibilities'.... This is such an obvious word to choose, that St. Thomas did just that, and gave the name of 'potential' to that sea of 'not-my-existence' and 'yet-possible-existence'. If a photo was taken of me with my hand at my head, I would have proof that I once 'existed' with my secondary act: my hand at my head. Which would be preferable to a photo showing that I once existed with another 'secondary act', another 'potential' or 'possibility': with my hand in the till.

Some of this created 'not-my-existence' (potential) surrounding me cannot possibly become incorporated in 'my primary act', my existence, but is itself not impossible to exist. I will never become a car or a fish. But there are other secondary acts which the human being <u>is</u> not as yet, or has not <u>done</u> or <u>made</u> as yet, but which he <u>could</u> be, or could do or make, or become, like making a car, or being a mother, or becoming a doctor. But it is important to realise that whatever 'secondary act' a human being will do or become, this secondary act will always be made up of these two components: what it eventually <u>is</u>: act (existence), and what it is <u>not</u> (yet). It is to this 'not yet' that Aristotelian and Thomistic philosophy wisely gave the name 'potential' or 'potency'. So the human being is capable of bringing forth secondary acts from the nature he received from his Creator, and from the 'potential' by which he is surrounded. And once the choice has been made, this new existence again is made up of what it <u>is</u>: the act (existence) eventually chosen, and that whole lot of what it is <u>not</u>: potential, or not-yet-existence from which it came, showing again that vast expanse of what he could have done or become instead, that is, to which he could have given 'act': existence.

A piece of marble is 'in potential' of becoming a sculpture; seeds are potential flowers or trees. Human beings are not only 'in potential' of becoming engineers, teachers, housewives, artists, but also of becoming children of God, or even Saints, sharing in the Divine Nature of God by Baptism! All the secondary acts are there to 'realise', i.e. 'to make real', to bring into existence, the potentials that the nature of this creature, the human being, is capable of. That is: to bring the 'actus primus' of his/her existence to perfection by choosing what is needed to become a good teacher, a good engineer, a good housewife, etc.

We spoke briefly of what is meant by 'not my existence', that, as a vast void, surrounds the primary act of human existence, and from which are drawn all humanity's secondary acts. But with his beautiful teaching, St. Thomas has transformed this void into a huge and plentiful ocean, brimming with all sorts of potential possibilities.

What an almost limitless panorama unfolds itself before us.

How richly endowed is man in his 'first act' of creation. His human nature in which he stands created 'in the image and likeness of God'; with his spiritual gifts of intellect and will, feelings, freedom of choice, memory, inclinations and aspirations. To that must be added the beautiful attributes that belong to his corporal and material make-up: his brain, the five senses, his physical strength and great endurance, his avidity to learn and master his surroundings, and his powers of recuperation and procreation: all contributing to an almost endless variety of choices and secondary acts, leading up to, if chosen wisely, the perfection of his primary act, the act by which he came forth from the loving hands of his Creator.

"The perfection of his primary act" we said. The perfection of his very own share in human nature. Here at last we have discovered the gold we are after. Let us polish it up so it will glow with the brilliance it received from God, before a grateful St. Thomas enshrined it as one of the crown jewels in his system.

The Divine Law 'dictates', that God lives according to the infinite perfection of His own divine Nature. In God there is no distinction between primary act and secondary act. God is infinite, unlimited, necessary and perfect Existence. God is all Act, which St. Thomas wisely calls 'Actus purus', Pure Existence. Existing is Nature to Him, and it is His Nature to exist. Since God therefore is necessary existence, there is no 'potential' in God, no becoming something He was not already before. The only 'potency' we may accept to be in God is that He is Omnipotent.

Divine Law demands that, at the level of Creation too, all secondary acts of His rational creatures are performed according to the nature of the Primary Act, and lead to its perfection. That is, that they make real, that they 'bring into existence' its glorious potential. God lives 'according to His Nature' which is unlimited perfection. As we saw, it is *this stamp* of God which is left on every rational creature that comes from His hands. It is this particular 'brand': to live according to the perfection of human nature, to perform secondary acts leading to the perfection of the primary act, which is left on every human being as the necessity, the dictates, of the Natural Law. Natural Law then is the human participation in the Divine Law. And the Natural Law dictates that only secondary acts are chosen which lead to the perfection of the primary act: human existence.

And it is right here, on the borderline between Primary Act and Secondary Act, that human conscience has its permanent home to secure this perfection.

Conscience is not the human brain. Conscience has immediate access to the human intellect. It dictates which secondary acts in any given situation will lead to an intermediate perfection of the primary act, that which is immediately required for the moment, and sounds a warning against secondary acts which would injure the perfection of human nature and might even impair human nature itself. Conscience has the power to arrest both intellect and will. The borderline between the primary act (human nature as created by God and given to a human person) and individual secondary acts is wholly subconscious. And it is conscience which makes known what happens on the border. This conscience is capable of doing, because it is in the primary act, that is in human nature itself, that the Divine Law: to live according to the perfection of one's primary act, lives as a permanent and indelible reminder. And it is the contemplation of any possible secondary act which triggers that living reminder into 'conscience': either by encouraging the choice of a good act or warning against choosing a bad act.

Conscience is not 'the voice of God' telling us what to do. When a car is being driven beyond the physical endurance of its 'primary act', it is not the car manufacturers who are telling the nut at the wheel how to treat the car properly: it is the screeching of the car itself protesting against the secondary acts to which its primary act is being subjected. In the same way, conscience is a safety device for human nature, an alarm that rings when secondary acts are being performed, or even contemplated, which violate the natural law: the human participation in the Divine Law, which says, 'that everything that exists must act according to the perfection of its nature, its primary act'.

Conscience can be overruled by intellect and will. Like the 'nut at the wheel' can turn up the radio to drown the 'voice with noise'. But until the total breakdown in hell, where the ruin of human nature will be fixed forever, this friction between the primary act and the wrong secondary acts will remain as a guide for both intellect and will.

[3] Once conscience penetrates into the conscious level, its message may be misinterpreted. This is especially the case with fallen human nature, where conscience has to cope with 'an inclination to evil', assisted by a host of unbridled desires. And then there are the already mentioned psychological, intellectual and moral influences in individuals, interfering with a calm and rational analysis of the conscience messages. And even if the poor intellect does understand, 'the flesh is weak'. Yet even if its voice has been dulled, a persistent uneasiness about a certain way of life is conscience's way of asking for an investigation and consequent further information. All this is one of the reasons why conscience can never be elevated to an absolute.

Is this not a beautiful way of seeing oneself finally confronted – following the speculations of philosophy – with the clear demand of Catholic Teaching: that ANY conscience needs to be an informed conscience! And it is precisely here that Thomistic

---

[3] This is the beginning of the section referred to in footnote 6, in the 'Note' at the end of this book.

Philosophy starts to "chime in with Revelation". For it is here, in the border region between the primary act and the secondary acts where conscience lives, that Divine Grace has its 'bridgehead' to assist conscience in its seemingly hopeless task to be heard in individual decisions, but especially in its long-term appeal 'for an investigation and consequent further information'. And was it not the purpose of this whole chapter to arrive at this juncture? And to come to a Catholic understanding of the 'mechanics' of this vital interplay? It is now possible to appreciate the fact that conscience, being a natural quality of the soul, capable of incomplete (and even erroneous) interpretations when it arrives from the subconscious through a mass of misinformation, is in need of the superior Light of Faith. In the souls of non-Catholics, Grace brings the blessed effects of this habit with it, because graces originate exclusively from the fullness of Grace and Faith within the Catholic Church. (Vatican II). [4]

Consequently, if any corrections are necessary, in order to make the human conscience an in-

---

[4] This is the end of the section referred to in footnote 6, in the 'Note' at the end of this book.

formed conscience, the corrections must - in all cases - be made with the superior Light of Catholic Faith. For a Catholic this means that it is almost impossible to be in 'invincible ignorance' with regard to an erroneous conscience, precisely because the superior Light of Catholic Faith is within him by means of habit, the supernatural virtue of Faith, and because of the known teachings of the Church. When non-Catholics, under the influence of the 'bridgehead': grace assisting conscience, seek further information, they too must be acquainted with Catholic teaching, because the graces helping them from the 'bridgehead' are Catholic graces, bearing the stamp of their origin.

Here is most appropriate to refer the reader once again to the authentic teaching of the Second Vatican Council, quoted in the Foreword of this book.

> "All men are bound to seek the truth, especially in what concerns God and <u>His</u> Church, and to embrace it and hold on to it as they come to know it .... The Sacred

> Council likewise proclaims that these obligations BIND MAN'S CONSCIENCE ..."

The Sacred Council refuses to give any latitude to non-Catholics in this vital obligation of 'seeking the truth'.

Finally, it is only Catholic Faith, surpassing human conscience, which has the final say in deciding whether secondary acts truly lead to the perfection of the REDEEMED 'primary act', of REDEEMED human nature: the knowledge and possession, in Catholic Faith, of the Blessed Trinity and all other supernatural treasures. Not just to take over its role, but to make <u>any</u> conscience perfect. For, as we know, it has not been given to any human power of faculty even to 'see' this, let alone to achieve it. And the human conscience, after all, remains a mere human faculty. Even when operating in non-Catholics, it is still operating in a redeemed primary act, thus relying on the assistance of the graces in the 'divine bridgehead', carrying with them the stamp of their Catholic origin.

On Predestination

Chapter Six

Catholic Teaching on Predestination

The Catholic Church's teaching on Predestination is not particularly tricky. In fact, it is pretty straightforward. Nearly all the trouble people have with this whole idea of Predestination seems to stem from the fact that it is viewed purely as a Revealed Truth. This is a mistake. For even though the extreme Protestant interpretation is repugnant to Catholics, they do not seem to know how to refute excesses in erroneous teaching on rational grounds, because they do not see their way clear as to how to tackle deviations from religious doctrines with rational arguments, even if they know by instinct that extreme Protestant interpretations cannot be true Revelation. This is yet another instance of the widespread ignorance of supernatural, revealed Truths, due to the deliberate eclipse of Thomistic Philosophy by the Modernists. The Modernists wanted this 'darkness of mind' and they got it! Well over a hundred years ago, they set their evil plans in motion to produce this ignorance and they were successful!

But – needless to say – the Holy Church was waiting for them, because of the very precise advance information, which 'Peter the fisherman at the helm of his barque' had received from the Pentecostal Winds without which the Holy Spirit has never left the Catholic Church since the first Pentecost Sunday. And the man at the helm in a number of Peter's successors sounded the warning in due course. And it is to be hoped that just enough faithful in the Catholic Church have understood the crisis and have taken remedial action.

The thrust of the new wind singing through the tackle of the barque was, that Catholic teaching at all levels must never be without the benefit of that magnificent handmaid: a thought system so powerful that "as by a pre-established harmony, it chimes in with Divine Revelation itself": the Everlasting Philosophy of St. Thomas Aquinas.

In the previous chapter of this little book we should have received an inkling of how necessary and helpful some understanding of St. Thomas' teaching on conscience is for the exciting knowledge of how Catholic grace (Vatican II) works in a human soul and conscience, and what the Holy

Fathers have in mind when they talk to us about this teaching 'chiming in' with Revealed Truths. It should thus not come as a surprise that, in obedience to this clear warning and teaching received from the man at the helm, whose task it is to interpret 'the winds in the tackle', that first we will view Catholic doctrine on Predestination in the steady light of Thomism, and from there we will let it 'chime in' with what we received from God on this subject in Divine Revelation.

The first thing to understand about this approach is that, if philosophy can study 'predestination' quite legitimately on its own, then 'predestination' must have a natural truth about it which makes it a proper object of a natural thought-system. And the second most important aspect of this whole approach is that, if a true philosophy discovers natural truths about its legitimate objects of study and investigation, then, what Heaven will have to reveal about it, will NEVER contradict what we already know about it, but will only lift the mind up to a knowledge about the subject which it was unable to arrive at by its mere created powers. But the truths discovered on earth by those natural means will be allowed to 'chime in' with the Revealed Truths in Heaven, Truths we did not know existed, and which we cannot arrive at or understand by our mere human powers, until God revealed them to us. But once revealed and given to the Church, we have been assured by the way ALL God's Revelation became known, that Revealed Truths will never contradict what we already truthfully know about the subject. "Contrary 'truths' cannot exist". Pope John XXIII in *Ad Petri Cathedram*, 1959.

We only have to look at the modern postal service, and in fact, at the whole elaborate mechanism of worldwide trade, to become convinced that sending goods and articles, and even human beings, on the road to a <u>pre</u>-arranged <u>destination</u> is as old as humanity itself. Because rational beings consider it a vital 'good', that these goods and articles and especially human beings arrive at their previously decided destinations intact after having been sent on their way by the sender, mankind has surrounded this whole elaborate activity of travel and commerce with laws and customs thought adequate for the protection of what is in transit. The fact that the sender relies so heavily on innumerable intermediate steps over which he has no control reveals, that the safe arrival at the other end depends essentially on the care and responsibility with which others exercise their free choices in the execution of their free wills.

It is only in trivial cases: 'taking the kids to school' or 'driving the bride to church', that we THINK that we ourselves control the arrival at the final destination. But even in these simple cases, how often has the siren of an ambulance reminded us of the truth that, with respect to arriving safely 'at our pre-arranged destinations', "we depend entirely on the care and the responsibility with which others exercise their free choice in the execution of their free will".

It is these two things:

(i) the fact that rational beings consider it vital that goods and articles, and especially human beings, arrive safely at their pre-established destinations, and

(ii) the fact that the safe arrival depends so heavily on the good-will of others, when things

> and people come under their care while in transit through all the intermediate channels, which Thomism picked up as the two essentials in its investigation into Predestination: souls in transit towards a pre-established destination in Eternity. We can be confident that these two truths will not be contradicted once Predestination is seen in the Light of Faith.

To get an even better idea of what St. Thomas will have to say about the essentials of predestination, let us look at 'a passage through time', which has been elevated to a much more spiritual plane, without as yet having gone beyond human practice.

Consider a mother who would dearly love her son to be a Priest. She is fully aware that she cannot take her son by the hand and drag him with her all the way to the bishop. So, like Rebecca in the careful execution of her dreams about her son Jacob, she becomes resourceful in her own wonderful womanly ways. She will watch over him when he is in her care. She knows his friends, his teachers, the books he reads, the company he keeps. She has direct knowledge of what she observes herself, and makes it her unobtrusive business to be informed of what others have to say about him. In the light of this knowledge she is always on the look-out for putting the right opportunities in his way without showing her hand by forcing him. When things at first do not seem to work out, she does not become discouraged. In her strong and devout heart she knows about the wonderful ways of God in whom she trusts. She is convinced that in all this she is doing His Will, and that, whatever her son becomes, he will benefit from the extra care she took in his youth to keep him on the straight and narrow.

This little life-story begins to lift the veil for us on the way the carillon of truths, discovered by Thomism as essential in any study on predestination, softly starts its pealing to 'chime in' with what we know of Predestination from Revelation. The mother sees it as a great benefit for her son that her boy should reach the desired destination. To that end she is not only prepared to take good care of all the intermediate steps under her control, but her diligence and solitude extend further to evoke the same beneficial influence from others, when her son is under their care during transit, without interfering with their own freedom of choice.

From the actions of this wise and resourceful mother we may learn, that the Priesthood was the mother's pre-selected destination for the boy and not the other way round: she was not predestinating the boy for the Priesthood. She allowed the final destination to influence her innumerable actions for the boy to make use of so he could reach the goal in life the mother had previsaged for him, as was the happy ending for St. Monica, and if the boy would eventually write his 'Confessions', as was the case with St. Augustine, then he would probably reveal how aware he had become in time, that he would not have reached his destination without the years of solicitude and self-sacrifice of his mother.

That human history is full of such stories of self-sacrifice of some for the realisation of their ambitious 'dreams' is very human and not necessarily Catholic. There are many instances in modern history where sections of humanity have been 'predestined' by their captors to a life of misery and premature death, but in all such cases this always entails the deprivation of free choice and the exclusion of the use of free will on the part of the victims. It is considered a heinous crime, especially if the selection of victims is totally arbitrary, as is the case in the taking of hostages. The barbarity against the Jews by Hitler and his Gestapo in the Second World War has forever branded this evil and mindless application of 'predestination' on the human conscience as 'a crime against humanity'.

We have collected enough information for the basic understanding of thomistic teaching on predestination. If we learn from the last-mentioned examples that pre-determining human beings to an enforced liquidation with the deprivation of the execution of their free will, is truthfully considered a crime on earth, then this truth will be upheld in Eternity. With this we can dismiss as blasphemy any idea of God 'predestining any human being arbitrarily to Hell."

Next, we must dismiss as equally absurd the idea that the foreknowledge God has of "who goes to heaven and who goes to hell" has the same effect as pre-determining the outcome. Not a trace of that was discovered in the philosophical analysis of predestination here on earth. God knows beforehand of every letter sent in the mail 'if it will get there or not'. If His foreknowledge of the letter's fate were the cause of that fate, it would be a truth discoverable by philosophy, and would be of such importance that it would chime in with Revelation. But mankind has never discovered this 'truth', and the Holy Church has never held it up as revealed. It would be the same as saying that God's foreknowledge of the Crucifixion determined the Crucifixion. If that was the case, then the Crucifixion would not have been a crime, and then Jesus would have been in error praying to His Father for the forgiveness of the grave sin the Jews and the soldiers were in the act of committing in crucifying Our Lord.

If God's foreknowledge pre-determines every human outcome on earth to such an extent that the utter uselessness of cooperating with grace would cause paralysis, then there would be no free will by which people could choose either to go with God or go against Him. It would mean that the Bible would be in error when it tells us with divine authority and veracity "that the human person is created in the image and likeness of God".

"I know my friend", said Duns Scotus once to a farmer, "that God knows beforehand whether this field will grow wheat or not. But if you don't put seed in the ground, I am afraid I have the same foreknowledge as God ..."

On the positive side, the safe arrival at a predetermined destination is considered such a great and vital good by humanity, that it has surrounded it with safeguards. The universality of this belief together with the inborn hospitality for travellers and even strangers, can only be truly a human good it is an echo arriving on earth from Eternity.

Next, the final arrival at a pre-determined destination here on earth depends essentially on the cooperation of innumerable intermediate agencies, all enjoying free will to either accept cooperation with the dispatch, or to withdraw from it.

Finally, the closest example of the true meaning of predestination on earth: the guidance towards a pre-set goal with the PRINCIPAL human will left completely intact, is found in the mother guiding her son towards a goal pre-set by her for him, by providing all sorts of opportunities for him to realise her dream of his priesthood. Here the 'essential cooperation of innumerable intermediate agencies' spoken of above is found in the way in which the opportunities are provided by all those interested in seeing the boy arrive safely at the pre-set destination, and for the boy to cooperate with them.

From examples like these it becomes clear to us, that God's foreknowledge of Augustine becoming a bishop or not is derived from His knowledge of whether he would cooperate with the opportunities provided for him from his mother's prayers and tears, or if he would not. If the foreknowledge of God would have been the sole factor determining the final outcome, St. Monica's prayers and tears would have been in vain: they would have had no influence and would have been idle against God's foreknowledge even of her own destiny.

According to St. Thomas, the Catholic doctrine on Predestination is

> 'that God from all eternity prepared the good works for the Just to walk into without forcing them to do so.'
>
> [Cf. S. Th. 3, 24, 1, c.].

This is in essential agreement with the two truths we discovered are inherent to human 'predestination';

(i) God cares about the safe arrival of human beings at their final destination: into His presence in eternity, and
(ii) He cares so much about this, that He surrounds every human life by predestining the good works to 'walk into': all the opportunities of 'safe conduct' by the innumerable agencies spoken of above. And all this tallies very well with the mother and all her 'helpers': the preparation of endless opportunities for the boy to cooperate with for the sure arrival of the priesthood (humanly speaking).

So, this is the truly 'Golden Mean' found by divine Providence in between the two extremes in every created intelligent life: no use of force, and no abuse of freedom in total license. Foreknowing all the circumstances of every human life that comes from His creative hands, He predetermines in advance all the good works for his creatures to walk into, to which are attached all the graces necessary for arriving safely at the final destination.

God is thus at once the Dispatcher, the Destination and the Means. He is the One who sends every soul on its way to its predetermined destination. He is the destination. And He is in charge of all the endless opportunities for arriving there, through the labyrinth of innumerable agencies meant to help His creatures on the way, creating for every moment of the earthly life of the soul the good works to walk into.

St. Thomas' definition says nothing of heaven and hell. It is completely silent on any destination at all, just as the mother concentrates on the intermediate opportunities for the boy, irrespective of whether he would become a priest or not. But, just as in the case of the mother, all the opportunities derived their efficacy from the fact that they were viewed in the light of the final destiny for her son, so too with the 'good works, pre-seen and prepared by God' for the Just to avail themselves of at every moment of their existence: they too bear the stamp of their final destination: union with God in Heaven.

God does not create the evil works for the unjust to walk into. They are entirely of their own making against the urgings of conscience assisted by Catholic grace. It is the refusal to walk into the good works provided by Grace, and to walk instead into the bad works of one's own creation by one's own decision, which ultimately leads to hell.

The Catholic Church's teaching on Predestination will not contradict common sense, as can be gathered from the foregoing. E.g. the Holy Church specifically rejects the proposition 'that some are predestined to life, others to death'. She teaches that God 'only predestines good works'. As for sinners, 'God does not predestine the evil works they 'walk into', nor the evil they do, only the punishment'. As for the just, God predestines both: their good works as well as their reward.

Still, for the human brain, some of the mystery associated with good and evil remains; but it is absolutely certain that behind the veil, NOTHING will be hidden that would contradict what has been said and taught all along. It is Catholic Hope that most of what remains hidden has a lot to do with God's infinite Mercy...

Before settling the question posed in the beginning, in the Introduction to this book, why the Catholic doctrine on Predestination must be treated with some urgency in this whole climate permeated with the poison of Modernism and the threat of the World Council of Churches, we must finish the foregoing by letting it 'chime in' with what God has revealed to us in Sacred Scripture. Since the whole stress of the Old and the New Testaments can be expressed in those two words: REPENT and from that blessed moment on PERSEVERE in doing good, it is not hard to find texts in which the transition from 'facing death' as a final destination to 'facing life' is clearly expressed. E.g. here follows a text from the prophet Ezekiel which is a clear indication of the possibility of going from one to the other <u>and vice versa</u>!

> "If the wicked man renounces all the sins he has committed, respects My laws and is law-abiding and honest, he will certainly live, he will not die. All the sins he has committed will

> be forgotten from then on; he shall live because of the integrity he has practised. What! Am I likely to take pleasure in the death of a wicked man – it is the Lord Yahweh who speaks – and not prefer to see him renounce his wickedness and live?
>
> But if the upright man renounces his integrity, commits sin, copies the wicked man and practises every kind of filth, is he to live? All the integrity he has practised shall be forgotten from then on; but this is because he himself has broken faith and committed sin, and for this he shall die ... Repent, renounce all your sins, avoid all occasions of sin ... I take no pleasure in the death of anyone – it is the Lord Yahweh who speaks. REPENT, AND LIVE."
>
> [Ez. 18:21-32].

'It is the Lord Yahweh who speaks' ... What can anyone say in contradiction to that?

One reference to 'the book of life' in the New Testament is in total agreement with this Old Testament reference to the reality of the 'fluctuations' between having one's name written in the 'book of life' or in 'one of the other books' as mentioned in Rev. 20:12, underlining the fact that 'this matter of life and death' is not settled until at the very last. I am referring to what Our Lord told St. John to write 'to the angel of Sardis'.

> "Those who prove victorious will be dressed like these, in white robes. I shall not blot their names out of the book of life ..." [Rev. 3:5].

In other words, it is possible to have one's name added to or subtracted from any list: 'It depends on you!' That, as we know, has always been the invariant teaching of Our Holy Mother the Catholic Church and is considered more important than solving the mystery of evil.

Epilogue

The reason why Our Holy Mother the Catholic Church for the last one hundred and twelve years or so (ever since the appearance of Pope Leo XIII's encyclical *Aeterni Patris* in 1879, to be precise) has stressed the overriding importance of St. Thomas Aquinas' 'Philosophia Perennis' is very easy to understand. NO heresy and no error live on the Supernatural Plane where only God and Revealed Realities dwell 'in inaccessible Light' [1 Tim. 6:16]. Unbelief and doubt most certainly threaten the Supernatural Gift of Infused and Catholic Faith but not by 'touching' it. It is killed only when the receiver uproots it. And the Catholics who do it, do so by accepting and believing a contradiction of Revealed Truth as true.

Contradictions, being errors, cannot live 'in inaccessible Light', and so the Divine Light of Catholic Faith is not needed to spot one. Contradictions are discovered by the light of the ordinary human intellect if not clouded by passions. And it is because the Modernists have done away with the BEST training a Priest can get in clear thinking: the Philosophy of

St. Thomas Aquinas, that modern heresies, errors and contradictions are not spotted, and so have been accepted by millions of Catholics at their peril. And when the ordinary human intellect accepts a contradiction as true, the Faith is at a disadvantage because it cannot take over the functions of a natural faculty. That is why that magnificent mind of Pope Leo XIII, trained on the 'Philosophia Perrenis', called the mind formed by this philosophy with such great precision and insight "the HEDGE of the Faith".

This must be seen as the reason why, in this little book, I went to the trouble to show how modern heresies contradict first and foremost clear thinking. Errors and contradictions in clear thinking clash with real truths ascertained by the human intellect. Only real truths will be able to 'chime in' with Revelation. Error and contradictions NEVER will.

Herein lies the crunch for all Modernists and for all Catholics who follow them. In rejecting truths which are ascertainable by the human mind, yet so beautifully connected with God's Revelations that "as by a pre-established harmony chime in with them", Modernists undermine Catholic Faith in Revealed Truths to such an extent that they end up disbelieving them! As that other great thomistic mind, Pope Pius XII, puts it in his 1950 encyclical *Humani Generis*:

> "The mind of man when it is engaged in a sincere search for the truth, will never light on one which contradicts the truths already ascertained. The christian ... makes sure that he does not lose hold of the Truth in his possession, or contaminate it in any way, with great danger and perhaps GREAT LOSS to the Faith itself."

The Modernist ideas on judging, conscience and predestination clash violently first and foremost with the findings of ordinary philosophy, and especially with the findings and the thinking of a system of such unassailable internal rigidity, that it is human thinking "chiming in, as by a pre-established harmony, with Divine Revelation". And the Holy Father who write that continues:

"No surer way to safeguard the First Principles of Faith."

'No surer way.' For a Pope, that really is saying something!

From this papal insistence we learn how the priceless Gift of Catholic Faith is undermined and ultimately lost. How cockle is to be identified from wheat. And why it is that the Modernists' own 'system', clouded over as it is by hatred, does not chime in with Revelation. Not having Thomism at its foundation, it is already ruined and vitiated at the ordinary human level of intelligence, deprived as it is of both logic and truth!

By preventing anyone from studying Thomistic philosophy and theology, the Modernists locked the door of true learning on themselves, too, and threw away the key. And so it is that their colossal ignorance prevents them from seeing that at the root of their own ideas on predestination (as was said in the Introduction of this book) lies as great a contradiction as lies at the root of Protestantism. By believing themselves and by teaching anyone else 'that salvation is secured', and that, 'in the New Covenant', everyone goes to heaven along his or her own path, they not only hold that everybody is predestined for Heaven, but also that Heaven <u>cannot</u> be missed. And here we see them "laying the axe to the Faith itself" [*Pascendi*, 1907]. For this flatly contradicts the findings of a three thousand year old philosophy: (i) that EVERY truly human secondary act has attached to it the moral obligation: that IN CONSCIENCE it must be performed for the perfection of the primary act in order to lead to its final end: union with God. And (ii) "that the obligation 'to seek the truth' binds man's conscience".

To accept a contrary 'truth' as equally true next to the truth is contradicts is not a secondary act which leads to the perfection of one's primary act, will not lead to union with one's final end, and so cannot be done 'in conscience'. In other words, it is immoral! Moral good and moral evil (the Ten Commandments engraved in man's heart) are already true philosophical principles 'chiming in with Revelation'. The Modernistic whittling away of moral evil to uproot the 'embarrassing necessity' of having to believe in hell cannot be upheld in Faith, because it contradicts an age old truth: God punishes evil. And contradictions do not chime in with Revelation but undermine Supernatural Faith in it.

> The Natural Law (the 'Ten Commandments') and its morality 'binding in conscience, to wit: that every human act must be JUDGED, in CONSCIENCE and in truth, in the light of its final end, PREDESTINATION: either leading towards it or going away from it, is one of the finest discoveries in nearly three thousand years of a magnificent human endeavour, a truly great Philosophy, reinforced in the Supernatural Light of Divine Revelation. Its denial is such an indisputable contradiction of fundamental human Truths that, according to infallible Church teaching, if the contradiction is believed, it will lead to the rooting up of one's Supernatural Faith in a Revealed Truth.

This is the way then, to finally bring out the organic unity between the three topics of this book: 'judging', 'conscience' and 'predestination', for the safeguarding of the priceless Gift of Catholic Faith, and for the uprooting of its gravest and meanest threat: the darkest blot on all human history:

Twentieth Century Modernism!

Note

For practical considerations what I wrote in one section [5] of Chapter Five, and what I subsequently wrote in another section a little later in the same chapter [6] could well be the most important pages I have ever written. The way Catholic graces, via the 'divine bridgehead', find their way into human consciences, whether Catholic or not, is the foundation of the Supernatural, Infused and Divine virtue of Hope. The Conciliar teaching of *Lumen Gentium* quoted in these pages serves admirably to reinforce biblical and dogmatic teaching 'that Catholic Faith is the foundation of Hope [Hebr. 11:1], as quoted in Chapter Four]. It is through considerations like these that we can nurture our virtue of Hope, when

[5] The paragraphs between footnote 1 and footnote 2.

[6] The paragraphs between footnote 3 and footnote 4.

we have to endure the test of Faith in having to 'believe without seeing'.

From FAITH in inerrant Catholic teaching we know (i) that invisible graces (including the ones we earn and merit) flow out continuously and exclusively from the Catholic Church; (ii) that they remain 'Catholic' graces, urging to Catholic unity; (iii) where they go precisely once they 'arrive' there: assisting conscience, which has influence on both intellect and will; and (iv) that we can depend on these graces, and how we can cooperate with them, in our dealings with others. In HOPE we trust that, if we persevere in 'walking into the good works prepared for us by Divine Providence', then these graces will be effective in the lives of all our dear ones, and in the lives of those 'entrusted to the priceless gift of our Faith'.

Whatever else I wrote I would like to be seen and judged only insofar, as an act of love, it helped and supported this vital understanding of the fundamental link between Catholic Faith and Hope, gained in the Light of Catholic teaching.

Thus it is, why the inerrancy of Sacred Scripture can declare "that only a child of Wisdom rules and must rule with confidence". [Wis. 8:14].

www.ingramcontent.com/pod-product-compliance
Lightning Source LLC
LaVergne TN
LVHW040220110826
845146LV00005B/1357
9798888705162